The Happitude
of Gratitude

EMILY
GRATEFUL FOR THE
TIME TO BRING TO
CAIL AND SO MANY
OTHERS

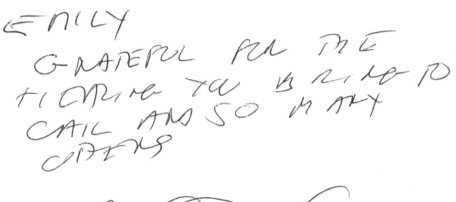

The Happitude of Gratitude

by Roy "Attitude of Gratitude" Kardon

ISBN: 0986258032

ISBN-13: 978-0986258039

DEDICATION

With love and Gratitude, I dedicate this book to my wife and soul mate Gail, sons Matt and Dan, my daughter-in-law Hannah, and most especially to my granddaughter Annabel. I am so Blessed to have you all in my life. The same goes to so many family and friends, both past and present. May I always be worthy of your love and affection as I feel for you all.

Above all I dedicate this book to the Sustainer of Life. Serving You is why I write this book, to be a light under those Created in Your Image. As I pray every day, Grant me the insight, wisdom, strength, and courage to do Your Will, and to help and inspire others to do the same.

Contents

FORWARD

There is a moment in the *Amidah*, the most central prayer of the Jewish tradition, that reads (in part), "*Modim anachnu lach*—We gratefully acknowledge You, G-d...for the miracles that are all around us, the wonder, the goodness in every moment—evening, morning and noon...."

Traditionally, this paragraph is recited three times daily–but as a Rabbi, I worry that too few of us actually pause to *see* the miracles, the objects of our wonder that are so worthy of our gratitude. Even for those of us who say the liturgical words, it is too easy to allow the wonders of our daily existence to pass us by, unnoticed. Life moves quickly, and the disturbances and annoyances are much noisier than the quiet, ever-present, self-affirming goodness.

That is why I so value Roy Attitude of Gratitude Kardon.

Roy is an inspiration, because he understands the Jewish value of appreciation—embodied in our prayers, in our blessings before even the most mundane of acts, raising those acts to deeds of holiness. And he has taken this emphasis on appreciation, and turned it into one of the most redemptive, uplifting regimens and lifestyles that I have ever witnessed. It is, truly, a model for us all.

He does not just say the words; he *LIVES* thankfulness. In every way, he "walks the walk" and has done so for some time, even before he wrote this book, which shows that he also "talks the talks." So like Roy—to *act*, before he talks about acting. But now that he has written it, we too can join him in his example of how to live a grateful life. This may be his greatest gift to us—a template for how we too can embrace an "Attitude of Gratitude."

I have never walked away from an interaction with Roy that has not challenged me to see the absolute best in whatever blessing or whatever challenge I next faced. His outlook and approach is transformative, and it is contagious. I pray that this book can invite others to see what a true *mensch* like Roy sees—the best in everyone around him.

For once, then, let US be the first to express gratitude – and say, "*Modim anachnu*—Thank you, Attitude of Gratitude, for sharing with us your secrets to thankful, fulfilling living!"

Rabbi Eric Yanoff
Adath Israel, Merion Station, PA
Kislev 5775 (December 2014)

INTRODUCTION

WHAT? ME?
WRITE A BOOK?

The date was July 31, 2013. It was early morning and I was to give the opening remarks at a Bisnow conference on the future of commercial real estate in southern New Jersey. I had given the same opening remarks for the same event in 2012 to rave reviews. That first time, I had used a fake phone call on my cell to describe how frustrating it is to do deals as a commercial real estate broker in a slow market (the market has picked up since). But in 2013, I messed up the PowerPoint and was forced to ad lib. I wound up forgetting to say a couple of things and thought I was just having a bad day.

Later, after I received a number of texts and congratulations on my speech, I came upon a younger man in his late twenties. He had the look of someone waiting for laughs. He told me I belonged at the Helium Comedy Club in Philadelphia performing at open-mike night. I told him he was very kind, but crazy. He persisted. In fact he looked so sincere about it, he convinced me to go online and check it out. While doing so, I noticed the Club had a class of four sessions. During the final one, you performed stand-up comedy on stage.

I told my wife and soul mate Gail that I was thinking of doing stand-up. Without flinching, she told me I was a better inspirational speaker than a comedian. Both ideas appealed to me, so I decided to try both.

I never seriously saw myself becoming a career comedian. And that thought was confirmed when I discovered how hard it is to become one. My performance was, however, highly received. I have since done four performances including two for Comics Verses Cancer.

The inspirational speaking idea stuck strongly, though, along with writing a book. For years I had done public speaking for the American Public Affairs Committee-AIPAC (the American pro-Israel lobby), ADL-Anti Defamation League (dedicated to fighting Anti-Semitism and all other forms of bigotry), and the American Cancer Society (ACS) to name a few. I had always loved public speaking, unlike the majority of Americans who apparently fear speaking in public more than they fear death. I figured I would write a book about my journey to achieving an *Attitude of Gratitude*, and then use it as a platform to get more gigs as a motivational speaker.

Hence the book you're reading now. It is the story of my personal journey to acquiring an Attitude of Gratitude.

The format of the book is that I describe how and why each major phase in my life has made me Grateful. The realization of my Gratitude for the episodes sometimes came years later, sometimes immediately. Much of it came with a struggle that I feel so Blessed to have experienced.

Gratitude can be expressed in many forms and toward many entities, people, or deities. Whatever way you express your Gratitude, I want you to know, is awesome. My form is simple. It is with the Holy One Blessed Be He or G-d. I use the last word of the latter sentence without spelling it out because I am Jewish and Jews are not allowed to write out the Holy Name. Although in recent years, many Jews have decided to write out the name for a variety of reasons, the Orthodox continue to use the form I just used. I spell it that way out of respect to my Orthodox brethren. It is my way of showing devotion and awe for the Almighty.

Regardless, in the most emphatic way I can say it, I intend this book to apply to people of all religions. There have been so many wonderful people of other faiths in my life who have meant so much to me as I continue along a path to be more spiritual. It is now my hope and prayer that whatever faith you are, this book will make you more Grateful. By becoming so, you will be happier and your loved ones will share that benefit, too.

Yes, I truly believe that the root of much of the unhappiness in the world is found in a lack of Gratitude. In fact, the reason I write about Gratitude with such a passion comes from observing conditions in our society that both annoy and sadden me. It is clear to me that people who are not Grateful, cause not only themselves but also those they care about profound unhappiness.

I first discovered the connection between Gratitude and happiness when I was in my twenties, when I travelled a lot for business. I was totally new to the business world and open to advice and guidance. On one of my numerous trips, a really nice, older gentleman sat next to me. We quickly took to each other, with him falling into the mentor role as he instructed a life lesson by describing what he had witnessed a couple weekends prior.

The man was on a luxury yacht his boss had rented out to impress some customers. After the customers had left, the people on the yacht docked beside them invited the remaining passengers over. The neighboring boat was maybe twenty-five feet shorter than the yacht his boss had rented, and had a couple fewer crew members. My seatmate went aboard and saw a man about my age sulking in the corner. The obviously privileged young man apparently was irate because his father had rented *this piece of [expletive]*, meaning the shorter boat and with fewer crew members.

My new friend wanted to make sure I never fell into the same category as the angry young man. We both agreed he was, in all likelihood, headed for major trouble in life. Not because of the shorter boat or crew, but because he was an ingrate of the worst kind. Nothing could ever satisfy him. He was clueless about being appreciative of all he had.

While I never forgot that story, the moral of it did lose its impact on me for a little while. Then a couple years later I met a woman who reinforced the lesson. I was working in an office building that she cleaned every weeknight. She'd come in and announce herself with, "hey hey!" Initially, I dreaded the sound of her voice because I wanted to get my work done and go home. However, that attitude quickly changed when we had our first conversation.

I had never met anyone so happy with her job or with life in general. In her dead-end, low paying, and what some would consider demeaning job, she found happiness. Her job allowed her to afford her home and to eat. She loved her husband, family, friends and neighbors. I learned from her that while a neighborhood could be impoverished and crime ridden, the people who lived there tended to stay there. The closeness everyone had for each other in her community was one great way to live.

That inspiring woman had an answer for everyone's problem, whether they asked for it or not. Most often, her advice made a lot of sense. But her insight about happy living was truly amazing: her Gratitude for apparently so little, never failed to bring light into my life.

The stories of the privileged, yet angry, man on the yacht and the happy cleaning woman are mirrored over and over in our society. There are way too many advantaged people who are not happy even though they want for nothing. Usually that is because they are not Grateful for what they have. In comparison, there are many with relatively little who find great happiness.

I am not saying everyone who is a "have" or a "have not" fits into those categories. I am just calling your attention to the power of Gratitude. I am trying to show you how a lack of it will doom you to unhappiness no matter how much you have to be Grateful for. Conversely, Gratitude can be found when you have very little.

The purpose of this book is to share my life with you. To depict all the struggles I have had and show how they all led me to look at life with an Attitude of Gratitude. The joy, peace, and love of people in my life have brought me happiness beyond my wildest dreams. It is my hope and prayer it can do the same for you.

*A*ttitude of Gratitude is a term I use so much, that I have proclaimed it to be my middle name. I even sign my name for people who know we well as: *AOG*.

I acknowledge that for all my struggles, I have been very Blessed from the beginning in contrast to many, especially if you compare my life to those of people living in many other countries. But it is my hope and prayer that by sharing my experiences, you will feel more Grateful for your life and every one in your life. While I would like to win a Pulitzer along with fame and fortune, if I can help you in your life I will feel fulfilled and, of course, deeply Grateful. We are all created in G-d's image so by helping you, I am helping Him. With your Attitude of Gratitude, I hope and pray you can do the same for others.

Thank you so much for reading my book and may G-d's countenance shine upon you and your loved ones.

HAPPITUDE

Happitude is a word I made up because I like how it rhymes with Gratitude, and I love how the title of my book sounds. And since it is my word, I get to define it. Wow! That's not bad for someone who truly struggled in every English class he ever took in school. Though my struggles were not as bad as the effect I had on teachers who contemplated a new profession after dealing with me as a student for one really long year.

Seriously, happitude means: *having a happy outlook on life and the people in your life.*

Writing this book has given me the opportunity to think back on my life and how I was feeling in many situations. When I do so, one theme seems to always come up: how I approached any life situation. Whether it's meeting one or more people; going to a party, event, or gathering; taking on a new task or assignment; or even meeting someone unexpectedly, the result from my point of view nearly always turned out to be based on the way I approached it. Yes there were times I was disappointed, even with a positive outlook. And there were things that happened way better than I expected. But, in nearly every instance, how I went into something is how I came out.

One thing happitude cannot prevent is tough times in one's life. We all lose people we love and care about. At one time or another everyone will have an injury or sickness. There are tough economic times, civic unrest, and business and professional setbacks we might experience. I think the goal each of us should have, is to survive and thrive the best we can. And that's what happitude helps me do.

Happitude does not mean ignoring when you should be sad or

depressed. To get over any setback in life you need to grieve in your way. There are some who, when they lose a loved one, will want to joke about it while another mourner may want to cry endlessly. Others want to think about normality, like when is their next golf game, concert, etc. When those situations happen, we all need give ourselves and others the permission to mourn, but not dwell. Happitude in those instances is about being upset and then fighting back by living life to the fullest.

Happitude can be found anywhere. Years ago I was driving on a long road trip with my sons Matt and Dan. There was an awful traffic jam. The radio said the tie up would last for a long time. My first thought was, *Oh no! What do I do with my beloved sons before they get crazy?* I responded by grabbing a football and getting us all out of the car to throw it around. I even took pictures of us "waiting." A couple other parents noticed and filed out of their cars. Quickly, the parents complained with sarcastic humor about the traffic. The kids asked each other about things like what team or player do you root for along with similar sarcastic jokes about the one thing that united us: how we all hate traffic. The traffic jam cleared and we got back in the car in a state of ease and calm, even a little joyful. To this day we joke about the incident.

Happitude can be found in anyone you meet. In the early years of being a volunteer chaplain, I went into a room with two patients (not the norm anymore) and found a shining example of this. The two patients were women about the same age with different, but serious, conditions. On my list was the woman who had registered as Jewish (I visit all Jewish patients and an oncology floor weekly). Upon telling her who I was, she responded by telling me to include her roommate in the visit. I could feel the beginning of a warm friendship developing between these two women. The woman who registered as Jewish stayed longer than her new friend. To me, this meant I got to visit her after the other woman had left. When I did, I found out they were communicating, even though they were no longer roommates. I believe they are still good friends today pending their medical condition. Having a roommate when you are in the condition both these women were, is normally a cause for stress, which is why hospitals are making single occupancy rooms. But these two wonderful women found a lifelong friend in each other and, I think, a great new support partner.

Happitude can also be found in the very mundane. In the Philadelphia area there are many Wawa convenience stores where I often go for lunch. If there is music I like playing, I am known to dance to it. I get some weird looks telling me many are thinking *what are you on?* I also get some smiles and, on occasion, even a dance partner. It brings me such joy. The workers there know me and always give me a smile. This makes a very routine activity a source of joy. Yes, if you see me in a Wawa, I would be honored to dance with you.

Another place I find happitude is my iPhone. I love music. Instead of watching news on TV, which dwells on sadness and the bad in people, I listen to music and think of the wonderful people and activities in my life. For news, I go to apps that tell me what is going on without all the negative hype.

Happitude is always a great way to deal with people. Often, the approach can take care of everything. Years ago I was at a long seminar that included an exam on the last day. There was also a group project that you were bound to do with strangers. The first day I was not feeling too well and had something stressful going on at work. My mood was awful toward the people in my group. The next morning an early phone call resolved the work problem and I also felt much better. I went to sit in my group's section, getting there (so I thought) before anyone else. I noticed I still had some paperwork on the problem. Thinking no one was there I said to the paperwork in triumph, "get out of here your *expletive*." Two group members saw and heard me, and gave me a look. I returned the looks with my triumphant story and extended my hand to give a high five. They cracked up with laughter and we became instant friends and actually stayed in touch long after the session. One said, "We thought you were a pompous *expletive*, not cool at all." Amazing what one's outlook can mean.

Unfortunately, in life there are many difficult people to be around. Happitude means you look for the good in them and try to find common ground. It's not always easily done. In those cases, try to limit your exposure to them and find areas you can either agree on, or at least get a chuckle from them. I once worked with someone who thought he knew everything. To humor him, I asked questions and acted as if he was telling me something new and brilliant. Doing so, made working with him more pleasant for everyone because he didn't feel the need to insert himself into every situation.

But, when you come across such people, do not forget to celebrate when they leave your life. I once sold a building to an abusive client who questioned everything I did and always had some criticism. I took a picture of the client at settlement so I could wake up every day for a couple weeks and look at it. It made me feel so good to remind myself that I did not have to deal with that client anymore!

May the Sustainer of Life grant you the mindset to approach your life and those in it with an outlook that brings you joy, happiness and gratitude: Happitude.

Chapter 1
WHERE DID ALL THE SMILES GO?

One of my earliest photos was taken when I was about one year old. In it, I am holding the hand of my maternal grandfather. Grandpop, as I called him, is helping me stand up so I could run. We are on the boardwalk in Ventnor City, New Jersey, where my parents had a summer home. The clothing styles in the photo are rather amusing now. I have a hat to protect me from the sun. Grandpop is wearing suit pants and a white shirt. You rarely see anyone in that type of dress during the summer months today, but back then, that was normal.

My memories of my grandpop are always of a loving, kind man. I think of him as someone who taught me what love is all about. Anything I did would be greeted by him with a smile, a big hug and a reminder of how much he loved me. Spending time with him at our summer home were the happiest times of my childhood. The photos all show me smiling with him, as in that early one taken of us on the boardwalk.

Unfortunately, that idyllic period would be very short lived. Around the time I was three years old, Grandpop developed stomach cancer, which would take his life in a little less than a year. Back then, the common practice was, whatever you do, never *ever* tell the children what was going on. While that was done with the best of intentions by my loving parents, it made me very scared and insecure. Why was Grandpop suddenly avoiding me? Why, whenever I asked questions about him, did I seem to upset my parents and my grandmother? Could I ever trust them again after he died at age 54 when I had no idea of him being so sick?

About a year after my grandpop passed, my father's brother was stricken with a brain tumor that would also take his life in less than a year. While I was not as close to my uncle as I was to Grandpop, I still adored him. He had a way of lighting up the room whenever he would come in or even if he just said *hello* to you.

My uncle passed when he was only 41. My father was very close to him and had spent many hours by his bedside, which meant he was unable to spend time with my sister, my brother, and me. It was a very difficult time in my family.

Additionally, seeing my uncle become so sick so quickly caused me to worry excessively about the health of both my parents. His death was made extra tragic because he was so very young and full of much promise when he passed.

Those two deaths in my family stayed with me for a long while and caused me to develop an assortment of fears. One was of the telephone. I learned to fear the phone whenever it rang. Back then, telephone use was not as prevalent as it is today. In my young mind, it seemed that when the phone would ring in our house, we received bad news. As a five-year-old in the 50s, I do not recall me, personally, using the phone. So in my mind, there was never any good that came over the phone. All the phone did was distract my parents and make them upset about something. At that time I also developed a deep distrust for doctors, too. I know that is normal for any kid, and it was probably even more so back in the 50s when painful shots were far more common. My distrust, however, came from their "failure" to save Grandpop and my uncle. Whenever I went to the doctor, I would think I better behave or he would let me down just as the others did for my grandfather and uncle.

Unfortunately, the deaths in my early childhood were not the only source of my insecurities. Shortly before my uncle was diagnosed with cancer, my brother was born. From the moment my brother came home, I knew there was something not right with him. As we would learn later, he has Asperger's syndrome, a form of autism. Today not only is there an abundance of knowledge about autism, but numerous support groups for family members. But back then, you were either normal or "retarded." My brother was neither. Sadly, he was not normal.

During my early childhood, his condition became a combination of a dark secret and a cause of great anxiety. Would I be like my brother if I did not do the right thing? Why my brother was that way and I wasn't, was a great cause for guilt. I couldn't help but wonder, what would my friends think of me if they ever saw my brother for what he was? Should I not bring friends over because they would think there was something wrong with me, too?

My brother's condition took a great toll on my parents, as all special needs children tend to do. The worst for me was not knowing anything about the disorder. Doctors (again, the villains in my life) told my mother that it was my brother's home environment that caused his Asperger's. If I had been older, I would have told her that the doctor was not right and that my brother was like that when he had come home from the hospital. Everyone's life in my family would have been brightened just to know what was really going on with my brother, to know that it wasn't his home that caused his disorder.

But, getting back to the photo of me at one year old, give or take, when I look at it, I see a happy child. However, from the time I was about three years old to maybe ten, there are few pictures of me having the care-free smile I had on that wonderful summer day. There was simply too much sadness, tragedy and struggle in my house.

The premature deaths from cancer of two family members coupled with being given a beloved brother with Asperger's Syndrome in many ways robbed me of a carefree childhood in my early days. Since I did not know any other childhood, I never questioned why I was given so much sadness and hardship when I was so young. But as more and more stories come out these days about childhoods haunted by too many forms of child abuse, economic hardship, homes of discord, growing up in tough neighborhoods, etc., I realized long ago that all the talk about idyllic childhoods are probably more a myth than reality anyway. There are many who have had far tougher childhoods than I did. The important thing now, though, is I feel blessed that my childhood came with gifts for me as I grew up.

In particular, my youth gave me was perspective on living today. As one who experienced profound loss at an early age, I learned compassion while young. Now I am lucky that I never forget how precious the gift of life is. Long before it became OK for men to hug each other, I easily embraced male relatives and friends in love and support. Similarly, telling someone you love them is something that has always come very naturally to me. I frequently tell Gail, Matt and Dan and many others that I love them.

To me, having a brother with Asperger's, is proof of how incredibly fortunate I am. My brother is probably the kindest person I know. When I once told him that a certain developer had purposefully bankrupted contractors building a building for him, he was puzzled as to why that developer would not pay if he had the money. He couldn't understand how someone could be less than honest. Yet he is incredibly bright. He can give you details of anything that interests him. He is also a true supporter of arts, which is something I know I should be.

My brother doesn't question, he just is. It is so sad for me to see him be a prisoner to a disease that makes it difficult for him to relate to people no matter how hard he tries. It is also difficult for him to talk about any subject he is not prepared to talk about, although his depth of knowledge and thought for anything he is ready to talk about, is amazing. But he is so kind, caring and sweet, that when anyone gets to know my brother, they love him.

In his pain, though, I feel such Gratitude for him being my brother. I always thought he would hate me because I was able to do many things that he could not. But he never held that against me. He is too wonderful of a person to do that. He was the first person to show me what Gratitude is all about, even if I did not realize it for many years.

I do realize that much of the anxiety and fear I felt as a child could have been alleviated by my parents or the doctors explaining things to me. But, in retrospect, I now understand the awful position the adults around me were in. Frankly, I am not sure what I would have told my children if we had been in a similar situation when they were so young. Thankfully, that tragic situation never came up and I now know my parents did they best they could at the time.

In fact, there are few of us, if any, who can claim a having lived a perfect, idyllic childhood. However, the most important thing to understand about your childhood is that it does not interfere with your adulthood. One common denominator among unhappy childhoods is that the victim is, in nearly all instances, not responsible for the problems. The most graphic and tragic example of that would be victims of sexual, physical, and even verbal abuse. I think nothing depicts that better than the wonderful movie, "Good Will Hunting." The movie climaxes when a psychiatric patient, played by Matt Damon, realizes that all his abuse in foster homes was not his fault.

So the question now becomes: *what is not your fault?* As we get older and farther away in time from our childhoods, we can often see the reality behind the experiences where we had erroneously deemed ourselves guilty. The truth is, you had nothing to do with a death of a parent or other loved one. And similarly, if your parents brought you into *their* failings in life, as if you had something to do with their problems, they were doing an injustice to you. You were not the cause of your family's financial struggles or any other struggle. Any elder who made you feel inadequate in any way, was wrong, in every way, to do so.

May G-d Guide you to let go of any undeserved burden you have from your childhood. May you gain strength to be a better and happier person through overcoming the weight of any unhappiness in childhood you may have faced. May this be a Blessing to you and your loved ones.

Chapter 2
THE CALM BEFORE THE STORM

Perhaps it only makes sense, that with all the tragedy in my life, I was unable to handle public school. I needed a more nurturing environment while I learned to deal with my fears and insecurities.

Thankfully, my parents did not accept the common mindset that claimed children should be seen not heard. They were sensitive to my needs and found a wonderful school for me, Miquon School. It could be called a number of things: a hippie school, a progressive one (remember this was the 1950s), a school without walls, etc. But for me, it was just what I needed. It spawned an era of growth for me.

Miquon was a place where your teachers were to be called by their first names only, which made them more human, less authoritarian in my eyes. I immediately felt comfortable being there, unlike in the public school where I had attended kindergarten.

Everyone was welcomed at Miquon. In fact, it was very progressive relating to social issues, such as integration. Between a quarter a third of the students were African American, which at that time was highly unusual. Not only were there many African-American students but I had three African-American teachers. In the late 1950s, early 1960s, that was not the norm. The multicultural atmosphere created a wonderful, accepting, non-judgmental approach for everyone. The message was: *consider each person for who they are as an individual and forget any stereotype*.

The main reason Miquon, for me, was very enjoyable and comfortable was the fact that there were no grades or tests. They used Cuisenaire rods, which are pieces of wood at various lengths, to teach math. I quickly became proficient in using them as well as anything related to numbers. Reading and English were another matter. I struggled mightily and did not enjoy either. But then along came a wonderful reading teacher who would later teach with my wife, Gail. She knew how to engage me by reading a sports-related book. It worked well enough. I became proficient at reading, but never very good at it or anything related to English. Later at Bala Cynwyd Junior High School, that would haunt me. At Miquon, though, it did not matter: no grades, no worries.

Miquon also loved to have you express yourself. That school gave me my first inclination that I am Blessed with a Gift to do public speaking. At Miquon, always with wonderful encouragement, I could speak up whenever there was the chance. When we had debates in class, if I could not convince my "opponents," I would do something dramatic to be remembered as the one who always got the last word in, even if it made no sense. That was allowed and encouraged. Don't forget, it was elementary school.

While Miquon helped me with my fears and insecurities, one of the things that brought me out of my sadness happened outside of school. It was professional sports. In the fall of 1960, I started following the Philadelphia Eagles. The first game I remember watching was at a friend's house with our families and a few others. The Eagles were playing the Cleveland Browns that day and won 31 to 29. The whole neighborhood was energized, as was school the next day. The Eagles, after a few years of being losers, suddenly were competing for the NFL Title.

The next game I watched was with my father, who was in bed for some minor illness. The game was so good, we still have that same TV. It was the game when Chuck Bednarik, also known as Concrete Charlie, knocked out Frank Gifford of the New York Giants during a thrilling 17 to 10 Eagles victory. They would clinch the NFL Eastern Conference title a few weeks later with a 20 to 6 win over the St. Louis Cardinals. Then, on December 26, 1960, the Eagles hosted the Green Bay Packers for the NFL title. The game, as was the common back then, was blacked out in Philly. But that was no problem for us. We were in Florida and saw every play of the Eagles 17 to 13 exciting win.

As the clock counted down that final game, we all screamed, "Go clock! Go!" Concrete Charlie held down Jim Taylor of the Packers and would not let him up until the gun sounded. The Eagles have yet to win another NFL (now Super Bowl) championship since. The Eagles are in the NFL East division, which claims 12 Super Bowls. Yes I can hear all you Cowboys, Giants and Redskin fans having a great smile at my expense. I will get you all back later with the help of The Pittsburgh Steelers and New York Yankees.

The next year, 1961, saw my sports fan-self become full blown. I started going to Eagles games with my maternal uncle and his friends. It was one amazing experience after another. The next day in school, I would always recall different curse words and the ways to show my emotions as an Eagle fan. The kids at school loved my performances.

That year I would also start following the Philadelphia Phillies baseball team. It was the year they had the longest losing streak (twenty-three games) in Major Baseball League history. They finished with 47 wins and 107 losses. Also that year, Wilt Chamberlain became my favorite player for the then Philadelphia Warriors basketball team.

One of the craziest idiosyncrasies I have to this day occurred at one of those Eagle's games in the early 1960s. I am now fanatical about not drinking liquids before or during any games. It took me a few years, but I finally realized that habit came from the fact that our seats were in the second bowl of Franklin Field and the only bathrooms were located on the basement level. As a ten-year-old, there was no way I wanted to go down there alone—nor did I want to ruin my awesome uncle's day at the Eagle's game. So at the first game I attended, I approached my uncle and told him I had "to go." It took him about a quarter and a half to take me. And that was not the worst of it: his friends never let him live down missing so much of the game Yes, he laughed about it.

Along with my affinity with Philadelphia teams, playing sports became vital to me and my uncle was the one to help me with that, too. He was often visiting at our house, always willing throw the ball around or shoot baskets.

Back then, the big three: baseball, football and basketball, were the most commonly played sports. And again, Miquon was perfect place for me to be—there were not many students, so I was always assured of being able to play in whatever games that were going on. With my knowledge of Philadelphia teams and my enthusiasm for sports, I felt I was part of the sports department at Miquon, though that department was technically nonexistent.

My sports skills were almost nonexistent, too. Aside from my uncle, I do not come from great athletic stock. My mother was always the last chosen for any sport and could not finish a 100-yard dash, which suited her fine because she never even cared to understand sports. We once went to a Phillies game that was tied after the ninth inning at 3 to 3. In the top of the tenth inning, Ron Santo of the visiting Chicago Cubs hit a three-run homer that would be the game winner. When my mother heard a home run had been hit she started to cheer. I shrunk in my seat out of embarrassment though we have a great time kidding her about it now.

Believe it or not, my father was worse than my mother when it came to sports. He described his football career as always looking up at the sky after being knocked down. After taking numerous golf lessons, his instructor told him that he'd heard my dad was a better tennis player. Trust me he was not. Not only was he not a great athlete, he hated sports. He would love ribbing me anytime a Philly team would win with something like: "Who did they beat? Miquon?"

To further annoy me, he'd bet me $5 on every Eagles game with a point spread. Of course, he'd take the other team. After the Eagles started winning, I would be up some money but would refuse to accept payment. I had more fun telling everyone how he would not make good on his bets. At his funeral I did forgive the debt. Doing so gave me some laughter on one of the saddest days of my life.

So perhaps naturally, my organized sports during my years at Miquon were the stuff that butts of jokes are made of. I played anyway, because I loved to. My favorite sport was baseball. Miquon did not have teams and there was very little organized baseball around, so I joined the Cub Scouts to play ball. Our team took the term pathetic to a new level.

We played nine games. Our best performance was a 10 to zero loss and the worst: 42 to zero. The latter game had two incredibly funny moments. The game started at ten o'clock in the morning and lasted for five innings. At one point, toward the end of the debacle, a kid on the other team said, "this game is going to be called on account of darkness." Even I had to laugh at that one.

I played first base for that game when our greatest moment came. With runners on first and second and no outs, their top hitter connected with a screaming line drive headed for our second basemen, who was playing with butterflies. My first thought was he was going to be killed by the line drive. Fortunately the ball landed in his glove so he could not drop it, even if he wanted too. The runner from first ran into him for the second out and the runner from second just assumed the ball would be dropped so he ran home. We picked up our second baseman and dropped him on second base for an unassisted triple play. It was the only inning we held anyone scoreless.

I have so very much to be Grateful for from the period of my life when I was at Miquon. For starters, I discovered what many American boys and girls also know: the love of being a sports fan. Discovering sports brought me many years of enjoyment as well as it helped me develop a sense of camaraderie. I discovered that when you know your sports, you will always have people to talk to and share a common bond with.

As far as my personal sporting career, I am most grateful for my uncle. While I could never claim the title of "Greatest Athlete" at school, my uncle's ever willingness to throw balls and play games with me gave me confidence. Now, as an endurance athlete over sixty years old, who recently finished 31 events in one year (including a marathon, Olympic Distance Triathlon, a 78-mile bike ride, and eight half-marathons), I know how Blessed I am to have the health to do it. As will be described later in this book, I have completed five full marathons, even though neither of my parents was into sports or fitness. My father was always amazed and proud of me, and I am greatly appreciative of his and my mother's support as I pursued my athletic goals.

However, my happy years at Miquon became the proverbial calm before the storm. While there, I thought of myself as a fine student

10

and an athlete. I figured I was one of those people who made friends easily, who was the lively student in many situations. But, as I will explain in the next chapter, "The Dark Ages of My Life," in many ways Miquon did not prepare me for the rigid world awaiting me at Bala Cynwyd Junior High.

For years, I blamed Miquon for what I saw as them failing me. I looked down upon those idyllic years. Yet, life experience has a way of helping you see things better. Now, I am Grateful to Miquon for helping me discover my gift of public speaking and showmanship. It was at Miquon I learned the basis of a strong math background. And my tolerance and curiosity for people different from me started at Miquon. I believe the school built my foundation for how I now perceive people as a Pastoral Care Visitor at The Hospital of the University of Pennsylvania (HUP). I now see people of all races, religions, nationalities, sexual orientations, socio-economic statuses, etc., as valuable individuals. I now love meeting new people and I always expect to find something great about them. In addition to being open to their new ideas and outlooks on life, meeting new people has made me very happy. I am always amazed at how much many of the patients give back to me, in spite of them being different from me in every imaginable way they can be.

Finally, Miquon's constant encouragement for me to speak up not only introduced me to my love of public speaking but it also encouraged me to become a very uninhibited kid in so many situations. In third grade they decided to make me, a Jewish boy, Santa Claus. I relished the role. I put a pillow over my stomach, donned a white beard and wore the red suit. On the day we had the Christmas show, I was on fire wishing everyone "Merry Christmas." People loved it. And not just the teachers but even the "older kids," the fourth, fifth and sixth graders did, too. I had no fear of going up to them and playing the role. Looking back, I realize that's where I developed the comfort level that would later enable me to make speeches like the one I gave on July 31, 2013, at Bisnow, and which subsequently led to my comedy gig at Helium Comedy Club, which in turn encouraged me to write this book as a basis for my motivational speeches.

One of the greatest feelings we human beings can ever have is to forgive and come to peace with the events, places, and people in our lives. I am not only at peace with my Miquon days, but I am Grateful for them.

Chapter 3
THE DARK AGES OF MY LIFE

Graduation day at Miquon in June 1963 was sunny and warm, the way I love weather to be. Each student received a special diploma with very personal information on it that brought a lot of joy to everyone there. There was love in the air everywhere that day.

Teachers came up to me to tell me how they would miss me. I felt a bond with virtually every student at graduation. We had grown up together since first grade. That summer I would go to Camp Robinson Caruso (no longer in existence) and had a wonderful summer with a large bunk of about twenty boys with five great counselors. We all got along so well, that even kids who, in other camps, would be the ones everyone picked on, were made to feel part of our bunk.

But as the close of summer approached and my days at Miquon grew further away, I became very sad and worried. What would it be like in the fall, at a new school?

The rumors I had heard about my new school, Bala Cynwyd Junior High School (BC), gave me good cause for anxiety. The principal and his deputy principal had a reputation for being very strict and anti-Semitic. I was told you always called your teachers by their proper salutation, Mr., Mrs., or Miss (back then there was no such thing as Ms) and that there would be homework and grades. Also, at my new school there would be no one from my Miquon days.

Giving me even more angst during the late summer of 1963 was the entrance into my life of detentions and suspensions. Apparently, they would be handed out at what seemed like the slightest infraction.

I felt terrified and alone immediately upon the last day of school at Miquon. Camp became an easy and enjoyable way to forget about the uncertain future I faced at BC. But from the moment I arrived home after that, I started worrying again.

Perhaps not surprisingly, the night before my first day of school I did not sleep very well. I knew a few kids in the neighborhood from dance class and other activities who walked with me that day, although I did not know them very well. My homeroom teacher was an old timer who liked to yell: "play the game!" I was bewildered by what that meant.

That first day we attended an assembly to meet our principal and his deputy. They were intimidating and to this day still I wonder how they ended up in education. They displayed a total lack of warmth toward any student who was not their ideal: that is, you received straight As (definitely not me!), were a great athlete if a boy or were a pretty cheerleader if a girl, behaved perfectly at all times, and, of course, held a faith other than Judaism. (That was 1963. I should say that when my son went to the same school decades later, it was a whole different story. The school was awesome for my son and so were the teachers, administrators and principal.)

During the assembly, we learned the very many rules we would have to follow. The first of which was that you were never allowed to chew gum. If caught, you were suspended immediately and it seemed your life would be over. Several kids swallowed gum to avoid this fate worse than death. But others were a little more sneaky. It used to drive me crazy when I would feel someone's gum under a desk. So much for how effective that rule was.

The gum was the least of our worries. Our homeroom teacher read to us all the causes for detention. As I recall, it took what seemed like an hour. I was afraid to cough for fear of being given a ten-year suspension for disturbing the class.

The sum result for me, a product of the gentle and caring Miquon, was to feel as if I had been sent away to the world's most notorious prison for life, run by the most sadistic men in the history of the human race. The harshness of my environment only encouraged me to draw even closer to sports. Sports immediately seemed like a way I could find my place in that foreboding institution.

On that first day of class, each teacher discussed the various teams that boys could to try out for. I heard three sports available: football, soccer, and cross country. I had been kicked in the shins early in my childhood playing soccer and I feared that sport because of all those bruises. I ruled out cross country because I was a slow runner. So I choose football, figuring that I was always a decent receiver in the pick-up games at Miquon.

The first day of football practice I followed in my father's footsteps and always ended up on my back. After one day, I saw the handwriting on the wall and gave up, rather than continue getting my head beaten in every day. The kids who were receivers were much faster and bigger than I was. Besides, there were only maybe five passes thrown a game, by both teams total, making being a receiver not even worth the effort.

By November, I added basketball to the list of sports to try out for. I figured I had a decent chance because at Miquon I was bigger than most kids and therefore I played under the basket where I'd get the rebounds and put the ball back in the basket. The first exercise we did during tryouts were layup drills. I got so nervous I missed about 10 of them. I did not bother to see who made the first cut. But I was inspired to do better. That spring I was determined to become a phenomenal ball handler. Unfortunately, after about a week of dribbling drills in my driveway, I realized the size of my hands made the practice a futile effort.

When spring came along, I gave baseball the final shot for my athletic prowess. The first day of tryouts I lost a fly ball in the sun and got hit where no guy wants to be hit. When I was up at the home plate, I swung so hard the bat hit my shins and missed the ball. Again, I did not check to see if I made the first cut.

The only thing that could have made me feel worse about myself and my nonathletic skills would be to go to the games. And of course, the rule at BC back then, was that everyone was expected to go to both home football and basketball games. I saw how far away I was from being anywhere close to good enough to make any team. With very few friends and being very shy and insecure, I would watch the games and wish it was me being cheered, or at least me being part of something, belonging to a team where everyone was friendly with each other.

Junior high was also the time when I became aware of girls. With my shyness and insecurity, I had no success in the romantic arena. A lot of crushes went nowhere for me. Often, during the games, I'd see girls I thought were cute cheering on the players and giving them coy glances and I'd think *if only I could be a better athlete, they would all want me.*

Having to do without sports was only one area to cause me unhappiness. My academic situation made things worse. I was completely unprepared for homework and the pressure of tests. Calling teachers Mr., Mrs., or Miss created, in my mind, a wall and foreboding sensation that they were all out to fail and ruin me. At Miquon, if you did not like a subject, it was no problem. You just made sure to do better in another. At BC no one cared about how you felt about *anything.* All they wanted was for you to do your work and remember that it was better to be seen not heard.

During the first Honor Roll assembly, our intimidating Principal coined a term I would hear at every such ceremony: "Why are you there and they are here?" When I looked at each honor student I felt totally inadequate. They all just seemed to come up with answers and great writing naturally, while I struggled.

My inferior feelings were borne out just after the end of seventh grade when I looked at the yearbook and was impressed by anyone who did an activity, especially sports. At that time I became what my family called a Walter Mitty, based on the character who daydreamed all the time in the James Thurber short story. In my case, I'd pretend I discovered a hidden talent in sports; one that would make me a superstar like maybe a pitch no one could hit. Other times I imagined growing a foot with total coordination or developing legs that would not be tackled while running the football. Of course, none of those thoughts ever came to reality. What came instead was summer camp.

The summer of seventh grade was the first time I went to a big-time sports camp whose name will go unmentioned. (I do not have great memories from when I attended camp there and do not want what I went through to taint other people's feelings for the place.) The camp was just all wrong for me from day one. Three days before camp started, I celebrated a birthday that would seal my doom. The

16

day camp opened was the cut-off date for age determination for bunks and divisions. Those three days meant I would be in the older, not younger, division. The consequences included a lot of time for me to spend on the bench, invisible, and being on the receiving end of some nasty, humiliating hazing.

That summer I would look with frustration upon the younger division (that I had missed by three days) when they played any sport near me. I would have been one of the better athletes on their teams. I would have been able to have friends who respected my athletic ability for the first time in my life. Instead, I tried out for every team or made myself available for any pick-up game. Without fail, I would be picked last and relegated to a position that would not hurt the team. When we would play another camp, I was allowed to go on the bus or sit on the sidelines, but never to play. No one would ever include me in any discussion regarding the teams. Yes, I was invisible, except for the hazing.

To make matters worse, I was one of only two new kids in the bunk that year. The other was a great tennis player whom everyone wanted to play, so no one bothered him. So I became the butt of jokes and had to endure bullying all the time. Camp for teenage boys back then, and in many cases today, was not fun for an outsider. I was subjected to chairs being placed over me while I slept, being teased with every joke imaginable and forced to clean all the dishes for our bunk's table after meals. The cleaning did not bother me; the humiliation was, to say the least, not much fun.

My life took a turn for the better in the summer of 1965 when I returned to that camp. I know you must be asking why I went back there if I hated it so much. The answer is twofold. First, I was embarrassed to tell my parents how poorly I was doing. Second, I was determined to do better. There would be a younger bunk moving up to my division. I got along with a few of them very well even though we did not see each other much. Besides, on the last night of my first year, one of the older kids in our division said to me, "Hey, come back. The second year you do not get hazed like the first year. You will be one of us." Since he had always been the nicest of the bunch, I decided to give it a try.

While my second and final year was far from perfect, it was

definitely much better. I learned a lot about tennis by pairing up with a friend from a younger bunk. We were evenly matched and had great battles, which improved our games. Most important, I resolved that summer not to be so laid back. I made myself start conversations to find out what would interest people in my bunk. Although I have no desire whatsoever to have anything to do with that camp now, I am Grateful that it helped me break a mold. I came back from it changed. I was no longer someone who meekly went into the corner waiting for his next bad moment.

Today I am actually Grateful for the tough times I experienced both at camp and at BC. In actuality, I know they are far more normal than I could ever have imagined back then. But because of them, I built upon the lessons I learned at Miquon and continued to grow and develop in ways that only do good for me now.

For example, there were two instances during camp and school when I learned how a kind word or act can really make a difference in the life of someone struggling. One happened the first day of seventh grade. On that fateful day, the students were expected to pick out who they wanted at their lunch table. The choices would remain for the entire year. No changes were allowed. Such a sensitive, caring administration!

As lunchtime approached, I became terrified I would have to eat alone and feel that degradation all year. I had heard stories of someone who had actually suffered that fate. I walked into the cafeteria feeling hopeless. But then, someone said one of the most beautiful words I ever heard: "Roy, sit with us." What a difference that made in my life!

The second time I realized the power of kindness when that older camper who had encouraged me to return for my last year. Not only did he help me come back to redeem myself, but he made my school year better. He had given me hope that the summer was not a total waste. Those little words helped me so much. Please remember you never know how much a kind word or deed can help someone.

So while both my camp and junior high experiences were painful, in many ways they were also an impetus for growth. The summer I resolved never to be too quiet or invisible ever again, I learned to reach out to people for the first time in my life. To prevent being the butt of jokes and hazing, I vowed never to act like I had it coming to me or as if that was what I was worth.

Today I never feel at a loss for words when meeting someone or being in a room of total strangers. I always find people to talk to and connect with. My athletic achievements (to be discussed in great detail later) are now admired by and inspire many people because I learned not to give up. While participating in numerous endurance sporting events, I seem to gravitate to those who are having a hard time. Often, these athletes are first-timers for whom finishing means so much to them. Because I have never forgotten where I came from, I reach out and encourage these awesome folks who are trying so hard. Many have given me smiles and personally thanked me for cheering them on. But I have fooled them all.

It is I who am so Grateful to see them accomplish something they never thought they could. I see them as versions of me in the seventh and eighth grade who suddenly become winners. I also know that some (not all, thankfully) youthful stars in sports unfortunately can never accept not being at the top of their game when they graduate. They all too often become overweight and out of shape because just playing pick-up games can never replace being scholastic stars. Fortunately, there are not that many of these folks but even one is one too many. I am grateful I was in the opposite situation. It's amazing how being a loser can make you a winner.

The resolve I followed through on to quit being meekly on the sidelines has paid off, too. Today, among many groups I am considered a very upbeat, happy person who loves being around other people. Few call me shy and none can believe I was ever shy. But for far too long, shyness often made my life worse than any of my shortcomings in both sports and academics.

One of the lessons I learned about shyness is that when you say nothing, others will nearly always have the wrong impression of you. At my ten-year high-school reunion, I noticed a classmate looking at me very seriously. After a while, she came up to me and demanded to know why I never asked her out. It was a great question because she was a girl I had found very attractive, but I had been too shy and insecure to ask her out.

In another situation, years after graduating from high school, I ran into a woman who was one of the most sought after by every guy in the school. But she had had a reputation of being a snob. When I mentioned high school to her, she related that she had bad memories because she was always too scared (a major reason for shyness) to go out with any boy. She had thought they all were only interested in her physical beauty and not who she really was. Happily, in college she put on some weight and suddenly was no longer every guy's dream girl. She then met a wonderful man who loved her for who she was as a person. She also lost the weight and still looked great.

Finally, I remember taking a business seminar after I entered the work force. We were assigned to do a group project together. I was very unsure about how I would fit into the group so I remained very quiet until I figured out how I could help. As soon as I discovered my place, the other people began to react very positively to me. Someone in the group told me, "Wow! I first thought you were pompous and aloof. You are too funny not to speak up all the time."

In other words, the result of my shyness was isolation that did not have to happen. And while it took a while for me to completely let go of my shyness, starting in ninth grade I burst out of my shell and started to really enjoy school (except for the work!). The fall of 1965 was the start of a new me. When I arrived home from camp, it was a perfect warm and sunny day: my perfect weather. I was looking forward to seeing my classmates again, making new friends and having some fun.

It's interesting how one of life's biggest mysteries that haunts humans is: why does so much personal growth come only after so much pain? Why not just give us the good without all the bad? I think the trick to answering those questions is to develop an acceptance that any problem you face, may just be what you need to grow.

I remember a great posting on Facebook or the like about someone's "conversation" with G-d. The person complained about an assortment of maladies that had occurred during the day. In each case G-d explained the "bad" thing was to help the human avoid a far worse thing. An example was: you get a flat tire so you would not have an out-of-control drunk driver kill you further down the road.

Think about how many adults owe their success in life to very strict, demanding parents that today they are forever grateful for, but in childhood often were deeply angry and resentful toward? As an endurance athlete in my mid-sixties, I have to do about 45 minutes of strengthening and stretching a day. In my sixty-third year, the day before the Chicago Marathon, I did my morning routine and felt so Grateful for all the times I had complained about having to do it because I knew I would not be at the starting line without them. How many people have turned tragedy into inspiration like the young child who loses, G-d forbid, a parent to a disease only to grow up to help find a cure for that illness?

Whenever something challenging and difficult comes into your life, try to step back and remind yourself that there just might be a silver lining. Look to anything positive in such a situation to help you get through it. Humor is often a great way to make it through the darkness of any circumstance you may find yourself in. And whenever you start on a journey that looks daunting, try to think back in your life to when something that seemed like a curse turned out to be a blessing in disguise, or at least was not as bad as you thought it would be.

May The Almighty One Blessed Be help you in any part of your life to have the strength to face it and the insight to see any light that will help you get through the darkness.

21

Chapter 4
ALL SORTS OF RAYS

The first day of school in the fall of 1965 was a Thursday. The sun was shining and so was I. We were in ninth grade, the oldest grade in the school! As I walked to school with friends, you could sense we felt on top of the world. I admit, for the first time in my life, I was a bit cocky. I had a feeling this might even be the year I joined a sports team. After all, I was one of the oldest in the school.

That day, however, presented me with another challenge in my academic life that was so great, it terrified me. They put me in the wrong section.

While I was far from a good student, this class was way behind me and the students in them were called some unsavory names by other students. I asked a teacher how you change your section. His rather curt response was akin to a death sentence: I had to see the anti-Semitic, mean spirited principal.

I convinced myself to just enjoy the easy year as best I could and forget about facing the monster running the school.

At the end of the next day, Friday, I asked a couple of friends at my table if anyone was doing anything on Saturday. I had surprised myself with my bold initiative and I was rewarded by being asked to join five other kids to go downtown to shop for records, cool clothes and good food. This was going to be my year!

Saturday started out awesome. I had so much fun. We talked about everything, eventually discussing our sections, teachers, and the kids in our sections. That is where the day went downhill. Upon telling my friends where I was placed, I was met by: "Kardon, they finally figured you out." I enjoyed the remark, as it indicated I was a part of the group.

But then I quickly changed my mind as they started to tell me, in no uncertain terms, that I needed to get out of that section because ninth grade counted for college. As the day wore on, I realized I would have no choice but to face the evil Principal, since my friends were threatening to tell their parents, who would eventually tell mine.

In retrospect, I appreciate that they were being true friends by caring about my academic future. But the following Monday I woke up to what I thought would be the worst day of my life. My parents had no problem writing the note, and I did not let on how I thought I would never come back to them after I went into the Principal's office.

My friends greeted me and demanded to see the note. They were satisfied and were very supportive but firm. They wished me luck and said not to "chicken out." I went to the school office and found the secretary to be very nice. She told me to wait. As I went to sit down, she said what I thought would be the last words I would ever hear: "He will see you right away."

I have no idea how I walked into his office but I did. I even managed to say, "good morning Mr. Whatever-his-name-was" as I handed him the note. He immediately became the nicest person I could have ever imagined. "Leroy," he called me by my formal name. "I'm so sorry there has been a mix up. We will take care of this right away."

He called in his Deputy and instructed him to take me to my new class. The Deputy, who we called his henchman, likewise could not have been any nicer. We actually had a pleasant conversation as he took me to my class.

From this episode, where I braved approaching the principal with my request to change sections, I learned to give everyone a chance and then give them the benefit of the doubt. Those two men, of whom I had spent two years living in fear, were actually warm and supportive that day. The less you have contact with someone, the more likely they will seem worse than they really are. I have seen this repeatedly in business negotiations; two parties will speak about their counterparts in the most negative terms until they meet each other.

As I looked around the room at my new classmates, I had a good feeling about the year and soon learned I was right. Instead of calling me *Leroy*, the teacher called me *Seroy* because he was unable to read my handwriting. The class cracked up, as did I, when the teacher made a comment about my penmanship.

I sat down and noticed the class joker giving me such a look, I had to turn away from or I would start laughing uncontrollably. As we went to our next class, he said my name would now be Delta Ray. His buddy disagreed and said Gamma Ray was better. Thus began my ninth grade year with the best class I would know in all my six years at the Lower Merion Public Schools. There were probably 20 or so names my classmates came up with. Among them were Beta Ray and Sun Ray. My various *Ray* names would be the cause for joking and good-natured juvenile fun all year long.

In essence, I discovered how much fun and how good at bonding silly jokes can be in your life. I am sure as you read the above you had nowhere near the laughter we did, if you found any humor in it at all. It is very much like telling a funny situational story and struggling to get anyone to laugh. It was one of those "you had to be there" moments that lasted all year. But most important for me, every time someone in the class joked about the Rays it was reaffirmation of the new bond I had formed with my classmates.

That year, for the first time in my life, friends would call me up or and ask me to join them to do typical things ninth-grade boys did in the mid-60s. Equally, I felt comfortable calling them to do a variety of activities like sports, going shopping, watching a game, etc. I was, and am still, so Grateful for this time in my life. To me I was out of my shell. I had finally finished adjusting to life without Miquon, and I was thriving in the evil world of Bala Cynwyd Junior High School.

And things only got better. Around November, as fall sports were winding down and it was time to go into winter sports, a friend suggested we go out for the wrestling team. At the time I had no idea what wrestling was except for professional wresting on TV. No one was really interested in it until he said we got to run the halls after practice. At that time, if you were caught running in the halls it was something like a week-long detention and a stern note home to your parents. We were intrigued by the prospect, but there was still the question about making the team. No problem. My friend assured us everyone made the team. Even *I* could make the team!

The first day of practice they weighed us and put us into weight classes. Afterward, we went to our weight class to find out who our competition was to wrestle for the right to represent the school in meets. In my class was a fellow ninth grader who was undefeated the previous year and another classmate who was far stronger than I. The latter teammate I thought I could possibly beat and have a shot at JV. But no luck. He pinned me in less than a minute.

The day still turned out OK because we got to practice moves and, of course, run through the halls afterwards. Besides, it just felt great to be on a team. Saying hello to teammates, whom I would not have known except for wrestling, made me feel a part of a team for the first time in my life. After two frustrating years of athletic failure, I was liberated so to speak.

Liberation or not, for the first two meets, I sat on the bench. Again, I was OK with it because I had a uniform on and I got to be part of the locker room for the first time in my life. We traveled on a bus, were excused early, and my name was on a roster.

When the third meet came, the coach told me I would be wrestling junior varsity. I liked the fact that instead of a six-minute match it was only three minutes. For those of you who ask why so short, you never wrestled before. It is a very exhausting sport. My friends and other teammates were wonderful wishing me luck and saying things like "get 'em Roy."

For some reason, I do not remember being nervous. As I stepped up for my match, I saw my opponent, who was shorter than I was and wider, but mostly in the stomach. I had a feeling this would be my big moment in sports. The match started and from the second we made contact, I knew I would win. In wrestling, if you pin, you get six points for first period and five points for every pin after the first minute period. You receive three points for a decision. I ran out of steam very quickly and was unable to get a pin but did win 6 to 1.

As I came to the bench, the coach looked at me in disgust and asked me, not too politely, how was it I could not pin my opponent. And my big moment was ruined. To add to my disappointment, we lost the match. I would wrestle twice more at Junior Varsity level, both times getting pinned in the third minute, almost able to secure a decision loss rather than being pinned. One match I thought my opponent wanted to torture me before pinning me.

The end of the season would be the end of my wrestling career. We heard the practice commitment for High School and all of my friends and I wanted nothing to do with it. Despite the fact that I had performed poorly in my three matches and had struggled in practice, I cherish the experience. Just being on the team was special to me because I was part of something bigger than me alone.

The 1965-1966 school year marked a major turning point for me. That year ended the "Dark Ages of My Life." Before that grade, I had always felt out of the loop in the social scene. Afterward, I would never feel that way again.

I am Grateful for my early social struggles because I now appreciate it whenever I connect to anyone in any social setting, whether it is business, charitable, or social. I also have a deep sensitivity to witnessing all people connect with others. I have found great joy at times when I least expected it—like when watching two friends give each other a hug as a greeting or seeing parents and kids hold hands or laugh together. I love that feeling and I feel Blessed to feel others' happiness. That joyful empathy had a great impact later in my athletic life.

That final year of junior high saw another shift for me, for which I am ever Grateful. Beginning in my ninth grade, my father became a great influence on how I relate to people in a very positive way. It started with the way he would his vent his "disgust" at my liking both spectator and participatory sports, neither of which he liked. It was a joke that turned into a great source of wonderful bonding between us that I dearly miss.

Dad loved to make fun of my wrestling team by calling it "wrastling." He told me about how he met a professional wrestler in the locker room once who was a friend of one of his older brothers. The friend was a local football player who would wrestle for some extra money whenever the show would come to Philly. The wrestling card my Dad saw was a tough one for the friend who was "pummeled" by the pro. When his brothers asked if he would like to go into the locker room, my Dad asked if the guy should be in the hospital. To my dad's shock, the friend was not only OK but also joking with the guy who had just beaten him "senseless." As the pro was leaving he asked the family friend to perform with him next time, adding how great he was to work with. My father used this numerous times to make fun of my wrestling in a way that only the two of us in our family could understand how much we loved this ritual.

His good natured teasing covered the entire Philly sports scene and it set the foundation of me being one who loves to "harass" people in a funny and friendly manner. That ability has been integral for me. I only want to get along with people and have learned to use my father's humorous style to defuse a conversation when someone disagrees with me on any political or other sensitive issue. I am forever Grateful to my father for this and so much more!

My experience in ninth grade was, in retrospect, very normal. Most kids have friends, are on at least one sports team in school if they want to be, and many sons have fathers to bond with over sports. What made these experiences so special for me was the contrast they made with my earlier struggles and the Gratitude I have for breaking out of bad times.

Whenever you are a part of a group of friends or share an interest such as a book club, running club, theater club, etc., with others, remember there are those who are not enjoying these experiences. If you realize that, you will find Gratitude for the blessing of being part of a something bigger than yourself and develop a sensitivity for those who are unable to find the same.

Chapter 5
THE WORST THING HAPPENS TO ME
AND RELEASES ME

In September 1966, I entered Lower Merion High School, the public high school in my area. Naturally, I was nervous about going from being among the oldest students to being with the youngest at school. But I had still had my close friends with me, so I wasn't alone. And even though the boys in my crowd were all suddenly interested in girls, we remained tightly knit. The girls in our sophomore class were more attracted to senior boys. So my crowd wound up hanging out together and dreaming about when we would start dating.

There were three major activities my friends and I regularly did. The first was we played a variety pick-up games. I was happy with that since my average sporting skills met with enough success playing among friends that I could enjoy the activity. Besides, making a high-school team was out of the question. The best basketball player in our pick-up games was cut the first day of school tryouts and wondered why he even tried out. Wrestling, as stated earlier, was a major commitment none of us were willing to make. I was way too small and slow for football, just like my father before me. And the pitchers in baseball threw way too fast for me to keep up with. So those pick-up games were perfect for me.

A second interest we had was professional wrestling, what is now called "sports entertainment." We loved it. Though looking back, I realize it was totally without any redeeming value except that it was fun. Professional wrestling is often deemed fake, which is very misleading. The correct word should be choreographed. Yes, the outcome is predetermined but it is still dangerous as all the stunts they do are painful and real. We would sit around the school lunch tables and debate who would "win" the next match. There was never any consideration given to athletic ability, only who would bring in more viewers by winning or losing.

The highlight of the year for us was when we went to a wrestling card with about eight matches. We walked through the crowd during the fifth or sixth match of the night and saw one of the combatants lose on a very controversial call. As he went to the dressing room he carried on in a tantrum, protesting his loss. The crowds booing him increased as he carried on. We passed the aisle he went down to the locker room and saw him reunite with his adversary where they both laughed and congratulated each other. I asked a friend, "Do you believe these people think this is competitive?" An angry woman came after me while my friends laughed hysterically. My laughter almost allowed her to catch up to me. Our love of professional wrestling would last all year. It was great for laughter and bonding with my friends. Girls would have been better, but you take what you are given.

Between the sports pick up games and the wrestling, I was a happy teen. So when we took up a third activity: Friday-night poker. It was the last place I expected to be where I'd realize my greatest fear: being compared to my brother. A little background is in order.

As I mentioned earlier, during the 1960s you were either normal or "retarded." No one had a clue about autism, so explaining my brother to my friends always caused me angst. What would I tell them? Would they link him to me? Would I need to defend him? I actually had to find an answer to all those questions during that first year in high school.

By the time we started playing poker, I had already stood up once for my brother. He was afraid of some mean boys down the street. so I took a walk with him to see who they were. My love for my brother was very evident that day. I was not exactly golden gloves material but I was ready to go to the mat against anyone for him. The mean kids turned out to be some boys who were younger than I was. I knew them, but not well. When they saw me with my brother they nodded as if saying, "Oh, he is with you. We will not bother him."

Unfortunately, the second time I faced a situation with my brother, it was not so easy. It turned into one of the worst things that could happen to me. And it happened during a poker night.

Poker was a game I was not at all good at. I am too honest and open about my feelings. As my self-given nickname Attitude of Gratitude suggests, I love to show positive feelings for all I am Blessed with. That does not play well in poker. One fateful Friday night we were playing at the home of someone who I thought was one of my best friends. Now that it is several decades later, I know he was just like me and everyone else: insecure and always trying to build himself up.

As I usually did, I made a bad move that caused him to win a big pot (the most you could win or lose at that time was, give or take, three dollars). As he pulled his chips away in triumph, he shouted, "Kardon, you are as dumb as your brother!" In anger, I picked up the table and tried to choke him with the end of it, knowing my friends would try to stop me long before I was able to kill him. Sure enough, they pulled me away from him.

I walked out of his house hurt and angry. The walk home was maybe ten minutes in a warm, damp evening. I was upset for attacking him but far more hurt that he would say something so awful. The worst thing I that thought could ever happen to me did.

I do not recall the exact events but do know my other friends (maybe I should say real friends) thanked me. My antagonist had been up. With me causing the chips to be thrown around, I accidentally made them all split the pot, causing him to lose some profits. As I recall, we did shake hands and apologized to each other. But our relationship would never be the same.

It would be unfair of me not to explain what happened to the two of us after high school. We did see each other a few times and were very friendly. Quite a few years later at a reunion we talked for a long while. He asked how my brother was in a very caring way. He is now living in Seattle and is a successful attorney. He loves the outdoor life and told me that if I ever come out there, we should do a race together, as he is an avid runner.

Some people talk about seeking revenge after being a dud in high school by returning a superstar. My revenge was forgiveness, which gave me the ability to look at a former enemy as one I could see myself being friends with. It feels so good to be able to do that. I am deeply Grateful for that reunion and the time we spent together. I wish him well and I know he feels the same way toward me.

It is said that making a friend out of an enemy has spiritual implications. In fact, it is the subject of Psalm 110, and in the New Testament, the Book of Matthew deals with it. I have even heard a prominent Rabbi discuss how vital it is and important to Judaism.

Of course, the forgiveness came decades after I had to deal with someone attacking my beloved brother *and* me. I had little to do with the attacker immediately after the incident. The rest of the weekend was spent with my other friends as usual, with no discussion of the insult or the fight, other than the dividing of the pot. And in school the following week, I experienced the most pleasant surprise I ever had: no one even mentioned it. As the days passed, I realized I had survived the awful attack and was doing fine. I did not miss my "friendship" with my attacker and I started to enjoy, and value, the company of my other friends a little more.

As I look back on what happened that night, I realize it changed me forever. I still feel the effects of that evening, but my perspective of my brother and my friends changed immediately. I stopped being afraid to bring friends to my house. When I would pat my brother on the back or joke with him, it is very clear that he is my brother and I love him. When I started dating girls the next year, I found my openness toward my brother was viewed in a very positive way. I imagined they would say to their friends, "Roy is so sensitive," but that did not matter to me. I was suddenly free of embarrassment and fear.

The episode at the poker game also changed how I looked at high school. Sure, I wanted friends and to be popular. And the next year, when girls became very important, I was like every other guy who wanted to impress the girls he dated or wanted to date. No one ever wants to be the person everyone else says is crazy or strange; the one everyone wants to avoid. But by that time, I knew I had real friends and I felt a lot more confident in myself than when I had first entered Bala Cynwyd Junior High School. That confidence gave me the strength to start thinking for myself and about what I liked, as opposed to trying to do what everyone else thought was cool. That confidence was also boosted by my father.

During my tenth grade year, my father, of Blessed Memory, became much more to me than just someone good for laughs who loved to "harass" me about sports. Being in the youngest class at high school was, at times, very intimidating. As, I would guess, all teenagers do, periodically I would become down on myself and feel the world was against me. I had a few moments of deep depression that elicited my parents to ask what was wrong. I described the circumstances (which were not really so bad at all in retrospect, but were the end of the world at that time) as my father would listen.

He never really had much advice except to tell me to think about what my friends were going through. That always made me feel better, as I would look at each of them and realize we were all in similar situations. But what really has helped me to this day, was one of his favorite sayings that he adopted from Jewish folklore: "for better or worse, this too shall pass."

That quote helped me then and still does whenever any bad or tough situation is upon me. As I look back on my life I can think of so many "disasters" that, really, were not so bad in the end. Eventually, they passed and I survived, always coming out of it for the better.

As I developed into a more confident and compassionate person during my typical tenth-grade struggles, I found myself turning more to G-d. Even though I did not care for going to Hebrew school, I was always attracted to G-d.

In Judaism everyone is expected to have their own relationship with the Almighty. Mine started in my younger days, single digits age-wise. G-d, to me, was a kindly old man with a beard who could show His love for me just by looking at me with great warmth. My first active memory of me thinking about G-d came during one of the space launches. For some reason, I thought we were all violating "G-d's World" by going where no one had ever been. While I know that was a juvenile understanding, I look back on the moment as my first realization that in exchange for the Gift of life we are given by The Sustainer of Life, there are obligations.

That sense of responsibility would often manifest itself by stopping me from being too mean at the times kids normally get ornery. I am not saying I was a perfect angel! I'm simply saying I recognized the importance of being good too all people because we are all created in the image of G-d.

During those awkward years in Bala Cynwyd and in tenth grade, I kept praying for The Messiah. Judaism teaches in the coming of the Messiah who will be of the lineage of David, the second King of ancient Israel. Christians, of course, believe the Messiah already came in Jesus Christ of Nazareth. Back then, whenever I would be in a pinch I would pray for the Messiah because, to me, the Messiah would be in the form of whatever brought me to happier times: a friend calling to get together, a good grade in school, or being successful in any situation. I know now that is not exactly what the Messiah is supposed to be about. However, it was the beginning of my relationship with G-d, and for that reason I look upon those thoughts with Gratitude.

Although I would hardly say my junior high school days and tenth grade were perfect bliss, I did get through them and grew because of them. As bad as things seemed to get, I never really suffered any permanent damage and I feel all the tough times made me a better person.

One of the methods of praying I did back then remains with me. I had often heard from Rabbi's, "G-d is where G-d is invited," so I learned to pray whenever and wherever the need came. My prayers were very personal. I did not need a prayer book, just some emotion or feeling.

I love that part of Judaism--being able to pray in your own words, whenever you want. I now think my preference for personal prayer has helped me understand and appreciate the Christian faith. I love to hear my Christians friends say: "praises to G-d" or "G-d Bless you." Occasionally, I even watch an evangelical TV program because I am inspired by the devotion and deep emotion found there. I also loved talking to Catholics who regularly go to Mass and describe to me their wonderful services like the ones they celebrate on Christmas Eve, Easter or Good Friday. Although it took me a while (as you will see in "Joy Amidst the Sadness"), learning to identify with people of other faiths has brought me much joy and contentment. We are all created in G-d's image and need to treat each other that way. And the foundation for me to understand that was laid during my sophomore year of high school.

About ten years ago, I went to a regional American Cancer Society (ACS) dinner to honor exemplary volunteers, which included two great friends of mine. The winner of the Courageous Spirit award was someone who became a great advocate for cancer patients with unusual cancers. When she, herself, was diagnosed with cancer, she forced herself to do what her mother had taught her as a young girl. That amazing woman went to her room and thanked G-d for the diagnosis. And that awful thing turned out to be a great Blessing in her life.

That inspiring woman touched me so deeply that I, to this day, try always to accept and be grateful for whatever G-d bestows upon me. When something is clearly good, like closing a big deal, finishing a race, or enjoying fun times with family and friends, it is easy to be Grateful. But I also want to be Grateful when circumstances appear to be anything that *but* positive, like an injury, sickness, losing a deal, or even when being treated not so nicely by someone using a profane name or two that I will not use in this book. I even want to be Grateful for things like bad weather or traffic ruining an event. There is no end to the power of prayer.

Upon hearing about the death of a loved one, Judaism acknowledges G-d as "the True Judge." Similarly, through the years I have seen many Christians accept the death of someone close to them as "G-d's Will."

Although the award winner who connected with me that night was of a faith other than Judaism, she touched me by expressing how ecumenical the importance of Gratitude is to all. Accepting something that, on the surface, appears to be bad is an act of faith. It

34

means you trust in The Almighty. And doing so will make you a more Grateful person for whatever you have in life. Therefore you will be a happier person who will make others happy.

I feel so Blessed to be able to share my passion on having An Attitude of Gratitude with people of all faiths.

May you be Blessed with the insight and strength to accept what is good as well as what appears not to be good in your life, in order to have Gratitude for The Sustainer of Life.

Chapter 6
YOU WIN SOME, YOU LOSE SOME

As tenth grade came to a close, my friends and I started to understand that dating would soon become a big part of our lives. The following summer, a group of us took a class in summer school. The class became cohesive and for the first time, my male crowd was hanging out with girls on a regular basis. We also joined a swim club where we all regularly spoke to girls. It was the wave of the future for me and my friends.

Eleventh grade started off as my best year ever. Suddenly, there were sophomore girls who were looking for upper-class boys. While they preferred seniors, juniors were just fine. My crowd had made friends with a couple groups from other schools and there were plenty of parties and other events to meet girls we could date. When we would walk the halls we could always count on seeing some girls who would give us a look or whom we could talk to in a very confident way.

Adding to being able to date was the fact that I could also drive. Suddenly, I did not have to walk to friends' houses for socializing; I could drive. Both my junior and senior years I drove to school and somehow always managed to find legal parking spots. The freedom a car brought was amazing. After school, I was no longer bound to staying within walking distance.

Dating was now the main activity on weekend nights. Afternoons typically were spent with the guys; evenings with a girl and sometimes guys and girls.

There are so many wonderful memories of Lower Merion High

School socializing. Lunch became a time to catch up on all the happenings going on in our ever-expanding world of LM and sports. In the halls in the morning, there would be numerous chances to hang out with both the girls and the guys and start the day off right.

LM sports also became a great source of enjoyment for me. I went to many games with my friends and supported our teams without having any envy at all for our athletes. I was content to be a fan and never felt like a failed athlete. We still had pick-up games for me to have flashes of athletic success, although not too frequently.

In short, life was good. I am forever Grateful for those times. For the six years I went to the Lower Merion public schools, I feel the Gratitude for me growing from a shy, totally insecure, isolated kid to being one of the gang. The joy of my last years there was recently rekindled at my fortieth- and forty-fifth-year high school reunions.

Although I have written a book, something not many can lay claim to, in high school I was a rather pathetic student. My wife Gail cannot believe my report cards. The word *underachiever* best described me. Whenever I actually tried, the results were very good. Unfortunately, I was rarely challenged to try, and that was really my fault.

When I went home with homework to do, I let other things keep me occupied. There were the telephone, sporting games on TV, or games I would come up with even if it was just using a marble to throw into a handle on a drawer. My sister has never let me live that down (and it would upset me if she ever did). On weekends when I should have allotted time to study, my thoughts turned to socializing, sleeping late, or doing something with sports—either playing or on TV. I had a lot of fun, but those activities did very little for my academic prowess in high school.

In addition to my poor study habits, I was not always an exemplary of good behavior in the classroom. In fact, there was an English teacher who I constantly tried to get the better of during my junior year. While something I can laugh at myself about today, it is not something in life I can say I am proud of. The lowest example of how I was toward her, was when she was called out to the halls with literally one minute left in the school year.

I used the occasion to say her nickname (not all that bad of one) along with some unflattering words. As she came back to the classroom, she heard the taunt and became enraged. But the year was over. To further prove my "victory" over her, I wished her a happy summer as if nothing had happened.

Turns out, it was I who was the loser. She had such a love of books that I should have capitalized on rather than be the immature teenager I was back then. During the school year she fell in love with the works longshoreman-turned-author, Eric Hoffer, wrote. We all made fun of her affection for him. But really, he was quite a phenomenal man. Instead of making fun of him, I should have listened to her and learned something. But as they say, the folly of youth was upon me.

As we approached the end of our junior year, it was time to start talking about college. At that time Montgomery County was pushing the newly founded Montgomery Community College. Students were desperately needed. When I met with that teacher to discuss my college choices, she told me I belonged in a junior college. I got the feeling she was just trying to fill the Community College's classrooms without my best interests close to her heart. But, since my grades were not all that good, my one shot at avoiding that fate was to work hard and perform well on the SAT's.

I know there is some controversy with SAT's and how they can discriminate against poorer students who do not have access to classes and tutoring. I didn't know about that then. At the time, I was just trying to get accepted into a four year college. Thankfully, I met the challenge and was able to look at several four-year schools and put the suggestion of going to Community College out of my mind.

In my youthful attempts to be cool, I had overlooked someone very special. That English teacher. Had I tried to learn from her, she could have given me a great love for books much sooner than I would find on my own. While I am there now, I could have had so much more joy much earlier. As one who tries to have no regrets, I do not have them with her. But I hope she is smiling down on me as I write this book and give her the long-overdue appreciation for how she looked at life. My relationship with her, though one way, has taught me to look at everyone individually as having potential for being in my life for a very special purpose. That understanding would help me in later life as I will describe in the "Joy Amidst the Sadness" chapter.

One of the greatest joys of high school was how my sister and I bonded during that time. As brother and sister growing up, we had our share of sibling rivalry. My sister is about a year and a half younger than I am. When she entered high school two years behind me, something magical happened. We found her friends were attracted to mine and vice versa. It was wonderful!

The two enemies became fast friends and have never stopped. As an aside, we have many laughs about that time, including how, when I was driving to school one day, the passenger door accidently opened when I turned. My sister fell out into the snow. She was not laughing then, but has ever since. It's just amazing how crazy incidents can bring you so much joy for so many years.

Regardless, after a couple months of dating I noticed a familiar pattern. There would always be a lot of thrill at first, followed by less interest whether on my side or the girls' side. I also started to notice that with dating, I took relationships very seriously. I was horrible at flirting and saying things that would lead to you-know-where. But back then, it was just before the sexual revolution, so probably what I said did not matter anyway. I always admired friends who could just "sweet talk" or romance really cute girls with no long-term intentions. Unbeknownst to me, I was already looking for that special someone. While you can all guess what was primarily on the mind of a 16- to 17-year-old boy, I now know in the back of my mind I was, and am still, meant for a monogamous relationship. As I will describe in "That's Not Right. Turn on the Lights," I was only three years away from meeting the woman of my dreams.

In the meantime, I never did "score" a lot. High school dating back then typically was filled with a lot of ups and downs unless you had a steady girl- or boyfriend. When I realized my pattern of behavior, I also found I would be very happy at the start of a relationship and very upset when it would inevitably end.

39

Two sayings got me through that period. One was my father's awesome *for better or worse, this too shall pass.* The second, as I look back was part of the foundation for my *Attitude of Gratitude.* It also permeated my many other activities when things did not always work out right, including LM sports. When anything went awry, I almost instinctively would say, "you win some, you lose some."

At the time the phrase was my way of trying to move on and recover from setback. However, that outlook has become a great Blessing in my life. I am very Grateful for it. By saying it, I was conceding some kind of defeat. But by using the words *win some*, I acknowledged that there will always be some wins somewhere, so I should pick myself up and keep fighting on. My later athletic accomplishments, in a lot of ways, would not be possible with the point of view that losses happen, but so do wins, so why not keep on trying?

Aside from dating, I became pre-occupied during my junior year on becoming my own person. Due to our family's business, my family was very prominent in Philadelphia. Adding to that prominence was the amazing success of my mother who was on her way to becoming a major player in the art appreciation/collecting/curator world. My parents lived a lifestyle that was legendary. But it was a world I never really wanted to be a part of. I was in high school with basically four areas of interest: girls, hanging out with the guys, rock-n-roll and soul music, and sports. My mom and I still love to kid each other about sports and the arts. Whenever I am able to guess who an artist is or make any comment proving I know a little something, I always add: "See? I am not just a shallow jock."

Although I always respected my parents' passion for the arts and their lifestyle, my goals were a little different. I wanted to fit in and be one of the guys and to find a hot girl to go with. Being from such a high-profile family tended to get in the way of that. I constantly heard comments about how rich I was. My house was adorned with valuable art that received rather strong notice from everyone who entered.

The fact that my mom was out working was also highly unusual. My high schools days were about two to three years before the women's movement began gaining national attention. Many parents of my friends were always amazed at what my mom was doing. Unfortunately, they were not as accepting of it as they would have been just a few, short years later.

Although back then I knew that my family led a very lavish lifestyle and the area I lived in was, and is, a very privileged area, I did not view myself as rich. And honestly, my mother working and my parents' lifestyle made me feel a bit like an outsider.

Of course there was, and continues to be, a silver lining to me feeling that way. I always have been so incredibly proud of my mother for all she has accomplished, as well as my father for supporting her. Growing up in that home helped me learn about couples working together and supporting each other. It also allowed my mother's immense passion for the art world to rub off on me. Not the art part, the passion part. While we focus on totally different arenas, it's with equal intensity. That's what I learned from her: *go after what you love*. Recently when I "complained" about how it was her fault that I do so many things I love, she replied with: "you can never do too much."

Yes, my mom is a shining example of a type-A gone crazy. I am forever in her debt for what she passed on to me. (It also gives me something to blame her for.) As we both laugh about it, I feel Blessed by how she is now giving all this joking to me. I can feel my father looking down, laughing with us.

So while my parents were happily entrenched in the art world, they still allowed me to find my own way. For that, I am Grateful. There were many activities they did with their friends that involved the entire families. Unfortunately for me, their friends were younger and had kids much younger than I was. But instead of insisting I come along, they would tell me to have fun doing something else and they respected the fact that I was not into their world. As the decision to go to college came closer, that perspective from them would be very important.

When high school came to an end my senior year, I felt the calling to move away and be my own person. The aura of the family business run by my dad and my mother's prominence along with the lavish

41

lifestyle, were something I needed to leave for four years in order to find myself. As we looked at colleges I was drawn to cities that were not too far from home, but far enough to have a place of my own. Boston and Washington, DC were the two that made the most sense. Eventually, I narrowed it down to George Washington University (GW) and Boston University (BU). I selected BU (without the fanfare of a highly coveted recruit). I was ready to make a break from the mold at home and become my "own man."

The last week of high school and that summer were both exciting and very nervous times for me. Although I wanted to go away, I was unsure about how I would do once I got there. No one in my inner circle of friends were going anywhere near BU. I would be on my own for the first time since seventh grade, or so I thought.

At that time I turned to my Judaism for help. I looked at the calendar and decided for both the major Jewish Holidays in the fall, Rosh Hashanah (New Year) and Yom Kippur (Day of Atonement) I would come home. Being in a school with close to a third of the population Jewish, that was not difficult to do, as many fellow Jews took the time off and some Professors too. For me, it was my way of grabbing some spiritual support during an uncertain time.

I had mentioned how beginning in my sophomore year I really began to pray in earnest and frequently. But that year, I didn't just connect to the faith of Judaism, I was beginning to connect to the concept of what it meant to be Jewish, to my whole heritage.

In that year, 1967, on June 5, The Six Day War started between Israel and its Arab neighbors. In the days leading up to the war, the Arabs stated their goal of "pushing the Jews into the sea." As nearly all my friends were Jewish at the time, we all were very nervous about the situation. I remember my mother crying, "That's the end of Israel!" in response to LBJ saying the US would remain neutral.

The war was a resounding success for Israel. Jerusalem was reunited, allowing Jews to pray at our holiest site, The Western Wall or Kotel as it is called in Israel, for the first time in many years. Another name for the Western Wall is the Wailing Wall to describe how Jews cried for centuries for not being able to pray there.

For me, the incidence was an awakening of my Jewish soul. Suddenly, I felt great pride in being Jewish. Fewer than twenty-five years earlier, the world had learned about the Holocaust, where over a third of all Jews were murdered by the Nazis and their collaborators. Now there was a Jewish state that could defend herself. I am forever grateful to the Modern State of Israel and for those who serve in the military there to protect it.

As I went off to Boston, my Jewish side began to emerge and my prayers were directed toward finding the good in things that were going on in my life. I felt that in order to deserve G-d's Countenance to shine upon me, I had to be a good person and do the good deeds the Almighty commands us to do.

At the time I did not realize something about G-d that had helped me then, and has done so ever since. G-d is Omnipresent and takes no form. G-d is where G-d is invited, as mentioned earlier. While I did not really comprehend those vital attributes of the Almighty, they helped me anyway. Until my high school sophomore year, I really had no idea how to pray other than to just talk to G-d. Those talks had helped me through so many insecure times during my freshman year. Whenever I would call out to G-d silently, as I do now, I have no doubt the Almighty is listening to me. The answer to my prayers may not always be what I want but I have found He has always helped me get through many tough times. Just like my high school saying, *you win some, you lose some.*

I went off to college with increased Gratitude for whatever was going well in my life and I remained hopeful for things that may not have been so good.

My Gratitude for high school was because high school was a bridge to me being on my own for the first time in my life in college. My decision to go to BU set me on a journey to discover myself: what I wanted in life and what values I hold dear. High school was also where I started to date girls and the beginning of my search to find the love of my life. That part would happen early my sophomore year of college. I find that search rather humorous now. I went to BU in part because there were more women and men unlike every college I considered. As it turned out, I met a local Philly girl before I ever really started to see too many college girls. Life is funny sometimes and since it turned out great for me, I am Grateful for that humor.

As a Pastoral Care Visitor, or volunteer Chaplain to be described in detail later, I have found many patients and their caregivers of all faiths looking to connect with The Sustainer of Life in the trying times they are going through. I have two suggestions I given my patients that they always seem able to connect with.

The first is the Omnipresence of The Almighty and His Openness to your prayer, however you give it. That message is do not worry about how you pray, just do it. Talk to G-d, think about what you want to say, or just cry about your situation wishing for help. I believe G-d will listen and in some way answer your prayers.

The second is there is always a way to reach for spiritual heights. So many patients of all faiths touch my soul when they describe what they are Grateful, for even when they are facing a painful way to a premature death. They have found a way to deal with their difficult situation with peace and grace. Talking about Gratitude has even connected with proclaimed atheists.

May you always know a way to pray and feel all you have to be Grateful for in your life.

Chapter 7
"THAT'S NOT RIGHT.
TURN ON THE LIGHTS."

The most important night of my college years actually did not happen in Boston, nor did it involve anyone from BU. As I did for the first two years at BU, I went home for the Jewish holiday, Rosh Hashanah. As the second day of Rosh Hashanah ended (Judaism, for certain holidays like Rosh Hashanah for Conservative and Orthodox Jews, are actually two days rather than one, due to Jews outside the Land of Israel being unable to tell when the Holiday ended so another day was added). The second day that year was October 2, 1970, the day after the last game ever played at Connie Mack Stadium. (Coincidentally, the last Phillies game at Veterans Stadium was also played on the second day of Rosh Hashanah in 2003.)

That night I had made plans with a close high-school friend to go to his fraternity house ZBT to drink some brew, hang out and watch TV. (We didn't have as many channel choices back then as we do now.) But my mother came to me with a crazy, grand fix-up scheme.

My first reaction was: "No way!" But then I quickly remembered that in Synagogue we said: "For the sins we have committed by spurning parents and teachers." So I changed my mind, said "yes," and made plans to take the new girl with me to my friend's fraternity.

To help you understand how much of a concession I had made to my mother, I'll briefly share with you the previous time she had fixed me up. There was some girl she wanted me to go out with so I called her. At that time, I had no trouble getting dates. While on the phone, the girl was a bit of a prima donna about the times and venues she was willing to go out with me so I told my mother politely, "thanks, but no thanks."

As I got ready to go out this second time, I let that first experience go. I was very relaxed and looking forward to a mellow evening meeting up with my high-school buddy's fraternity brothers. At eight o'clock, we drove up to pick up mine and my friend's date. I knew the other girl well, the one who would be the date for my friend, and I thought they would get along just fine. No worries there. Mine was the wild card.

But when the door opened and I looked at my blind date, Gail Helene Friedman, I thought she was perfect. As we walked back to my car, I kidded about my driving ability and how we may not get there. She laughed with me. I could not believe how comfortable and great I felt to be in her presence.

When we got out of the car to walk to the frat house that night, I reached out to hold her hand. She put her arm around me and I followed suit. It was my night!

We talked the night away, breaking away a couple of times for some kissing and hugging. We stayed up until three in the morning. I dropped everyone else off first before driving her home where she made me knockwurst, a head of lettuce, sour kraut and other delightful foods. The following Sunday we went to the West River Drive in Philly, now named Martin Luther King Drive. (As an aside: Dr. Martin Luther King, Jr. graduated BU, too.) Gail came over to dinner that night before I took a flight back to Boston. As I kissed her good-bye I said, "Now I have something to come home to." At that time Gail was sixteen, I was nineteen. She was a senior in high school and I was a big sophomore in college. Yes, I was robbing the cradle.

The interesting thing is: meeting Gail almost never happened. Her friend had suddenly decided she did not want to go out. She had turned the lights off figuring we would show up and leave with a dark house and no answer. Gail, always being the considerate person she is, thirty seconds before we arrived said, "That's not right," and she turned on the lights.

I truly believe the hand of G-d was there that evening, making sure I would meet the love of my life. In Hebrew this is called, *Kol Breshet,* which means it was meant to be.

When I returned to BU, Gail sent me a very innocuous letter and started what would turn out to be a lifetime of phenomenal communication. With it, she put in a piece of aluminum foil that she said was from the Connie Mack Stadium. For the first of many times, she fooled me, eliciting a great laugh that I am sure the guys in the dorm wondered where it came from.

I sent her a letter back that was likewise, not too deep. Then, Saturday night, October 31, 1970 rolled around and that changed everything. Remember back then the only two ways you could keep in touch long distance was via telephone (very expensive) and snail mail. On that fateful night, I was about to go out with some friends to a Halloween party. But my body told me I was going nowhere. A week later I flew home and was quickly diagnosed with mono. That meant a lot of staying in bed with a very painful sore throat and very little energy, except to call Gail.

Those conversations kept me going for about six weeks. After that, I finally felt well enough for her to come over. After nearly two months of dreaming about her, I got to see her again. We had a great time and I felt even closer to her.

At the beginning of December, I went back to Boston to try to salvage the semester. The first day back I walked to class and had no energy to write any notes. I went to the bursar and told them my situation. They were very understanding. They told me to go back home, rest up and come back for the next semester. They withdrew me from all courses, meaning I wouldn't receive an incomplete or other penalty. (Though, that also meant I missed out on an automatic A. As I would discover later from a fraternity brother, the school failed to provide a projector for the exam, so the professor gave out As. Opportunity lost!)

The second semester didn't start until late January, which gave me close to two months to recover and get even closer to Gail. About a week before I had to go back to BU for the second semester, I was driving on a very cold, damp and dreary day. Elton John's "Your Song" (Gail and I had said that would be our song) came on the radio and I realized that for the first time in my life, I was in a relationship with a girl that I could never imagine saying good-bye to, or "let's just be friends."

Gail would come up to Boston for a few weekends that spring, making them the best times I had in Boston. Even though she was much younger (she was a year younger than her class to begin with), she always knew how to relate to my friends. She has always been someone who could fit into any social situation with beautiful grace. My fraternity, ZBT formerly Phi Sigma Delta, had the most amazing spring weekends. I was always proud to bring Gail. I still am today.

Part of Gail's charm is she has the ability to remember everyone she meets. Whenever we go anywhere in public, she always sees someone she knows. Our kids never liked going shopping with her because inevitably she would run into someone she knew and would stop to talk. The ultimate example, though, was the celebration party for Philly Fit in 2009, as will be discussed in "My Championship Team," when Gail knew the first person we saw at the party. The group was comprised of amazing athletes and people who lived a significant distance from our neighborhood. Perhaps not surprisingly, at my twentieth high-school reunion Gail saw two people she knew. What was surprising, was a classmate of mine then asked me my wife's name, not mine because she seemed to have always been part of the group. That night Gail was probably the only spouse or partner in my class who did not go to my high school, who had no trouble finding people to talk to.

As a couple we have had our share of challenges in life, just as everyone has. We endured losing a family business and having to start over and re-invent who we are, especially me as I found other work. It was hardest on Gail as she had to work her residential real estate as a serious player. While she has been incredibly successful, the non-stop high-stress nature of her business has been difficult to say the least.

Our first four years together were under the brain tumor that her beloved and wonderful father Victor Friedman suffered. Those four years were at the end of the course of disease that took him from us ten days before his 49th birthday. He had survived the Holocaust but not cancer.

Like everyone else, we have had losses and dealt with loved ones struggling with various ailments. Our respective work sometimes made things difficult, too. But what makes being with Gail so special, is we go through it all together. We do not look to each other to change anything about the pain we may be going through at the time. No matter how much someone loves you, that person cannot take away your pain. He or she can only help you get through it. Gail and I rely on each other to be sounding boards and each other's greatest fan. That is what helping someone you love is all about.

As I look back on why we are so happy I see humor, respect, and kindness. We love to laugh and make jokes about nearly everything. We also have many comedy routines such as Gail hiding my food when I am not looking. When it comes to being romantic I am the leader. Our running joke is Gail saying super mean and nasty things to me with a straight face either in private or in the company of a few family members who laugh with us. Crazy thing about that is we are always both horrified whenever we hear other couples talk to each other in the same way but totally serious. As it has turned out, in a few instances we find those couples actually get along just fine. We are just so sensitive to each other. When it comes to helping each other we both make extraordinary efforts to do so and view it as normal, not as a sacrifice. That is what love is all about.

Yet in many ways, we are very different. Gail is far neater and more organized than I. Trust me; she has told me that more than once! But we do share very important, similar feelings on ways we look at the world. A few years ago someone I know was jilted by a man just before they were set to be married. He also stole just about all her money. I gave her a couple hundred dollars and wished her well. When I told Gail, without any hesitation, she told me the woman could use the money. Gail has done likewise with other people, and I always tell her it's a good way to spend our money with an approving hug.

Even when either of us is angry or upset with people, we usually do not show it very well. I have seen Gail meet with someone who gave her the short end of the stick (you can use the vernacular if you like) and still talk to them. Gail will say she was mean to them. But the reality is, she is always respectful to them. I, too, am very bad at

49

keeping grudges or animosity.

As I will describe in later chapters, I do a lot of volunteer work. There is no way I would do so much had it not been for being married to Gail. Whenever someone she knows is in trouble, particularly with illness, Gail draws them closer. Others may draw away, but not Gail. I am so Grateful to be married to her. I can hear her saying to me something like "speak for yourself!" as we both laugh.

More than being my soul mate in so many ways, Gail helped me calm down and become a man. Although I had helped her through her beloved father's illness, when I met Gail I was neither very secure nor all that mature. I saw in my future, me going into the family business that, at the time, was one of the more prominent, private businesses in the area. I was a mediocre student and while I had plenty of friends at that point, I was hardly a leader. In short, I was average, facing a daunting task of being the next generation in a family business that was well over 50 years old.

The success of my parents seemed like a mountain I could never come close to climbing. Gail quickly became the foundation in my life. I know I could always count on her for emotional support. I could feel her confidence in me before I had a lot of it myself. Gail also loved me for who I was, not for what I was trying to be. Early on in our relationship, I realized for the first time in my life that I felt completely comfortable around someone when I was just being me. I shared a lot of my innermost thoughts and fears with her and every time, without exception, she said it was OK. Whenever I would have a tough time with anything, Gail was always there to pick me up with whatever I needed.

Gail's family situation was far from easy street. As I mentioned, her beloved father was dying a slow, painful death. Her family's business was a store in a high crime area that her mother had to run when Gail, her sister, and brother were still in school. In addition to being responsible for the store and dealing with her father's terminal illness, there was the emotional baggage from both of Gail's parents being survivors of the Holocaust. At that time the Holocaust was only beginning to be discussed. In the years to come, there would be numerous films and books about this human tragedy brought on by human inhumanity to fellow human, anti-Semitism, and other baseless hatreds. It has only been within the last few years that the effects on both the survivors and their children from going through such horror have been recognized. It is something that never really goes away. At the time I met Gail, no one knew or discussed the issue. By supporting her, I, in so many ways, grew up very quickly.

In the circles I had traveled at the time, the main goal was to have fun and be carefree. As I supported Gail, I found myself leaving that world and putting others' needs ahead of mine. In many ways I was being true to myself by doing what I cared about most for maybe the first time in my life, even if it was not the fun thing to do. Caring for that special someone was where I wanted to be.

In retrospect that period was the start of feeling the best part of who I am today. One of the many benefits I get from my volunteer work is it makes me feel important and powerful. In "Joy Amidst the Sadness," I describe my work as a Para Chaplain/Pastoral Care Visitor or volunteer Chaplain. In that role, I am always amazed that my prayer and/or presence can provide light for those suffering as well as their loved ones. Those early years with Gail were the commencement of the journey that led me to doing that wonderful Ministry. As I could feel myself being able to help Gail, subconsciously I started to feel useful and powerful in the ways that matter most in this world when all is said and done.

I have said about my involvement in the fight against cancer through the American Cancer Society (ACS), "from the worst things, the best things come." My life changed in so many good ways by helping the love of my life face the way too premature death of her father. Of course, I would have preferred something different and have her father be around today, but in life we do not always get to make those choices. The choices we have are how we respond to those situations. Then those choices often define us and make us who we are.

During that sad time with Gail, I would learn a lot about

supporting those going through a serious or terminal illness of a loved one. Only in recent years has the impact that those situations have on caregivers and family been understood. From my work as a volunteer Chaplain and life experience, one thing I know for sure is that everyone reacts differently. I remember being in a prospective clients' office as his beloved father was on his deathbed. He told his daughter, "I do not care what you do," in response to her question about seeing her grandfather one last time. As he put down the phone, he explained that his father was in a coma with no chance to come out of it. He remained at work to honor his father. The business owner explained how proud his father was that his son had a successful business, so why not work? His daughter had been very devoted to her grandfather and had been by his bedside a few days before and told him how much she loved him just before the grandfather sank into the coma. What at first seemed callous, that the man remained working, was in fact a loved one dealing with his grief.

To those of you who may be going through a period of grief, I am sorry for your loss. I know that phrase, taken word for word, may not seem comforting, but it is the proper way to greet someone in mourning in most instances. At a recent house of mourning, I greeted the mourner with that sentence. His eyes brightened as he thanked me for being honest. It seemed everyone else was asking how he was, or telling him he'd get over it.

When you go to a house of mourning many wonder *what do I say?* Your presence says it all. It says you care and are there for them.

To those experiencing loss, feel free to be sad in your way. May your happy memories of your loved one help get you through this difficult time. To those going through this together, understand we all do it differently. Be supportive of each other and try to respect how each of you deal with grief.

These lessons have helped me deal with personal loss as well as being supportive of other's going through loss. Remember also there is no happy potion to take that will help anyone in the long run.

As I went through that early tough time with Gail, I could feel myself growing, as well as us growing as a couple. Again you do not choose what may happen in your life, only how you respond, which ultimately defines who and what you are.

May the Sustainer of Life Comfort and Guide you.

I am very Grateful to be married to Gail. I have been in numerous situations in business where a group of men start to complain about being married and often tell jokes about their wives or marriage. Everyone laughs but me, because I have no idea what they are talking about. And I learned a long time ago not to try to joke with them because there will be no sincerity with it.

The Gratitude I have for Gail being my wife and soulmate is unending. Being able to go home and always be happy to see her and vice versa (even if she will never admit it!) to this day brings me such happiness and inner peace. I could not imagine living any other way. The way we talk and treat each other bring such light into everything I do. Many say I am always so happy. The answer is look who I am married to.

Chapter 8
LEARNING THAT THE COLOR OF THE WORLD IS GRAY

When I had first left for college in September 1969, I had no idea how profoundly I would be changed during my tenure there. I was primed and ready to figure out who I was and what kind of man I would become at the same time the United States was experiencing one of the most turbulent times in its history. The main issue of the day was the Viet Nam war. Young men my age were being drafted to go fight a war that was, to say the least, not particularly popular. That summer a man landed on the Moon, proving to us that nothing was impossible. And Woodstock took place, the ultimate symbol of youth rebelling against "the system."

I think one of the first things I discovered about myself at college was that Philly wasn't the only city I could love. One of BU's attractions is its proximity and convenience to the great city of Boston. While the Boston Celtics might easily be the team I hate the most, I love Boston. I am so in love with the city that I'll intentionally speak with a Boston accent just for fun. I even kept contact with someone in business just to hear that Boston accent. BU is in a great location to take advantage of the many things Boston has to offer, which I did as much as I could.

On campus, I explored the ideas and movements that fueled much of the student activity. Some were easy to accept and become involved in. For example, the first thing that autumn that everyone seemed to get involved in was protesting and ending the war. It was easy to see why: at eighteen, all the males were draft eligible but had a student deferment. The last thing anyone wanted was to graduate and be forced to go to Viet Nam. Many I know went into teaching after college to avoid the draft, only to leave as soon as the military became all volunteer. But ultimately, the real reason we protested was because we, like many Americans, were asking, "what are we doing over there?" and no one was answering.

President Richard Nixon also made for an easy target of us students. Great bonding and a lot of camaraderie came with the protests. Big demonstration days took the place of big sporting events, even for me.

But I didn't just blindly follow movements. One fall day a couple friends and I were in the student union when Students for a Democratic Society (SDS) took over the building in protest. As I recall, they were striking against GE. I was in the business school and found myself automatically questioning what their protest was about. I had no problem with SDS against the war, but the union being against a company did not feel right. As I read the pamphlets, I became even more opposed to that protest.

My friends, many fellow business students, agreed with me. We started making fun of the hypocrisy of many of the demonstrators. My inability to accept such radicalism became even more evident when I got to know a new perspective from my freshman-year roommate. He was totally radicalized and seemed to think the so called revolution was right around the corner. He was very optimistic about his value to this revolution. But he did not seem to have much of an answer about how the revolution would feel about his stereo, tickets to concerts and the fancy motorcycle he was riding.

I did not ride him too hard, but I did decide his ideals would not be a good match for me. As time would go on, several friends of mine would enjoy making fun of the radicals. Yes the war was bad. We agreed to that. But not the country as a whole, or our system in total. Just a few changes were all that was necessary, we decided, and all would be OK.

It's interesting to note that while I was figuring out that I could trust my government while acknowledging it wasn't perfect, I discovered something quite shocking about it. At one point when I was home with mono, I was down in Gail's basement waiting for her to get something. While there, my eyes were drawn to a book by Arthur D. Morse, *While 6 Million Died: A Chronicle of American Apathy.*

As the title suggests, it was a horrifying account of American acquiescence during the Holocaust. On the front cover was a big picture of FDR with his smile, smoking his signature cigarette attached to a long, narrow holder. My family, being made up of a solid majority of Liberal Democrats had put FDR up on a pedestal. That groundbreaking book detailed how he, the State and Defense Departments, along with a heavy anti-Semitism undercurrent in the US at the time, conspired to make for a weak and disgraceful response to the Holocaust. I was totally shocked. I had thought the Holocaust just happened, that no one could have done anything about it.

I began to read more about anti-Semitism and as I did so, I kept asking myself: "Why do they hate us so much?" I reasoned that since the world is generally messed up, there must be something good to Judaism.

As I continued to learn about anti-Semitism, I also questioned my faith, which led to me re-solidifying my connection to it. My perpetual search to understand what Judaism is to me, remains both constantly life changing and ever evolving.

There are several facets to Judaism that I love. First and foremost, I appreciate how all of us are encouraged to have a personal relationship with The Almighty. One can pray at any place and any time. As I mentioned before, "G-d is where G-d is invited." And whenever you do a Mitzvah, which can be translated to mean you follow through on a Commandment from G-d, you are naturally drawn closer to G-d.

Also in Judaism, everyone is important. I love the Jewish law that says in order to make a Minyan, the quorum required to hold communal prayer services, you need ten Jews. The Orthodox hold it must be ten men, all other movements are fine with including women. The equality of the value of all human beings is found in the fact that ten of the most humble people count for Minyan, but only nine of the greatest Jewish scholars are not enough.

We also believe that all people are created in G-d's image. Human life and the value of each life is delineated in an important phrase from the Talmud: *"...whoever destroys a single soul, he is guilty as though he had destroyed a complete world; and whoever preserves a single soul, it is as though he had preserved a whole world."*

There are a few anti-Semites who tried to say this only includes Jews, but the fact is, it is about *all* human life. The way I like to say it is that we are all G-d's children. We have so much more in common than what makes us different. That understanding of the sameness that unites us all started for me during my college years.

Originally, when I began studying Judaism in earnest, I figured I would become Orthodox. That would entail keeping Kosher, or following the Jewish dietary laws, which is also called *kashrut*. Some of those laws include eating no pork products or shellfish, and no mixing meat (including poultry). You are also forbidden to do anything work-like for about 25 hours during the Sabbath from Friday Night to Saturday Night. That time is supposed to be set aside for rest and spiritual enrichment. In other words: no driving, no watching TV, no turning on of lights.

Keeping so strict to the Sabbath was not something that worked very well for me. I confess: I find it hard to stay still. I love to always be doing something. What has always worked for me, though, is prayer. I love to pray and now I pray pretty much every morning. I find it helps me focus on what I need to do to serve G-d and figure out what G-d wants from me. It is also a time I find myself becoming more dedicated to the people in my life. I truly believe we serve the Almighty by serving those created in His Image.

At BU, while I was still developing my sense of Judaism, I discovered there were only a few students who spent a lot of time in Synagogue, or any other house of worship, at least among my circle of friends and acquaintances. So my solution was to pray every Saturday morning. I had a tallis (a Jewish prayer shawl) and prayer book to go along with a yarmulke. I would pick out some prayers that were important and then go to pray for a half hour or so.

Toward the end of my prayers in the book, I would add my personal prayers. My personal prayers, while asking for something, always recognized there had to be a reason for me to be granted something from The Almighty. Almost by instinct I would say something to the effect of "to do the Will of G-d."

Many times I would ask not to be embarrassed or not to fail at something like an exam so that I could better serve G-d. In my mind, I couldn't understand why would G-d grant me something simply for my pure enjoyment? What use was that to anyone or G-d? But, if passing an exam meant I would be a little happier and therefore better to others, I reasoned that would be justification to pass the exam. If I would be able to have a great time at a party, my enjoyment could be contagious to others. That was a major moment, an epiphany for me regarding my relationship with The Holy One Blessed Be He. During my Saturday prayers, for the first time, I realized I had responsibilities to Him; that things were not provided just so I could take and take.

In Rabbi Abraham Twerski's *Living Each Day* (given to me by my sister-in-law), there is a story about how G-d would look at prayer. If you keep asking for the same thing, G-d might say, "here we go again, asking for something purely for themselves." In this wonderful story the person praying just wanted to be closer to G-d. The rhetorical question is this: *whose prayer is dearer to Him?*

When I realized I would not be Orthodox, I searched for methods that would remind me of G-d every day. I chose to keep Kosher, the Jewish dietary laws explained above. Although I did not follow the laws regarding using different plates and utensils for different foods or for eating only under Rabbinic Supervision, I did eat only kosher meat and poultry and did not mix dairy products with meat or poultry in the same meal. I followed those rules for close to 15 years before I broke away for a few years. My rationale for the break was *why should I deprive myself?* At the end of a few years, though, I decided it was important to keep the Kosher style that I had before, with the exception that I would eat non-kosher meats and poultry (but not anything such as pork or shellfish that could never be kosher). I also do not mix dairy products with those meats and poultry. I have done this for several years and feel very stable with that observance.

My form of keeping kosher, my *kashrut*, is not common for Jews. Usually, you either do or do not keep kosher. Most Jewish Americans do not. For me, I do it because it reminds me of serving G-d every time I eat so it works for me. Numerous times when I plan how to eat and observe my *kashrut*, I find myself thinking about The Almighty and how I need to always be kinder, more patient, more considerate and just a better person. For that reason, I remain very committed to my form of *kashrut*.

Upon renewing my commitment to being a Jew and a more spiritual person, I started following more than just sports in the world. Perhaps naturally, I became more interested in my religious ancestry and heritage. During my junior year, in the summer of 1972, I went to Israel for the first time. The trip cemented the beginning of a deep love and pride I have for that amazing country. The amount of medical, scientific, technological and entrepreneurial advances from that small country is astounding, especially when you consider it is all done in an area of the world that, for the most part, does not recognize its right to exist. I find it tragic that Israel's Arab neighbors continue to try to destroy a country that has so much to offer. I realize that some people say Israel is an apartheid state, but that's not what I experienced. During my tour, I saw many Arabs and Jews living in harmony back then when, if you look at Israel's enemies, you'll frequently see apartheid practiced every day to anyone who is not a heterosexual Moslem man.

Another issue that caught my attention when I was in college was the plight of Soviet Jewry. Three of my four grandparents came from some part of the then Soviet Union. Speaking in general, Russia's history is one of the most tragic of any country when it comes to individual lives. I am Grateful that my ancestors were able to come to the awesome country of the USA. In fact, my gratitude was so deep, that while at BU, I felt a sense of responsibility to get involved in trying to free my brethren in the USSR. While I was far from a leader in that movement, I did become involved in protests and some organizing.

The era was the first time I started thinking about human rights and how it relates to me being a Jew. The human right of freedom is integral in my religion. In fact, Passover is a holiday to celebrate when we Jews were freed from slavery. Freedom is the basis for being able to choose to be a Spiritual person. If you live under a dictatorship, as tragically too many do today, your decisions in life are made for you, including spirituality. It is only when you are free to do whatever you want, that you can choose to do good works and become a spiritual person.

Please do not get me wrong. I was far from a perfect student or person in college. I joined a fraternity, Zeta Beta Tau (ZBT), formerly Phi Sigma Delta, and had my share of carefree collegiate life. At times I was more than a little out of control, and I engaged in plenty of self-indulgences. My fraternity brothers and I, as well as other friends, for the most part ever since have had success and are decent good people. But youth does have its way of showing itself as it did for me and my friends.

Regardless, a great lesson I learned as I became more involved with the world is that not everyone shares your opinion on everything. As I would debate, in friendly ways, with friends about the issues of the day I began to realize that they had their good points even if they disagreed with mine. The key element in those discussions was respect for each other. Of course there were occasions where someone's views were, in my mind, a little too much. But I quickly learned to avoid those discussions for a simple reason: they were not fun. Besides, I knew I could not change them just as they could not change me. The main thing I learned is if you find common ground on something else with that person, you can get along just fine and feel good about them and vice versa. Too many people today demonize the other side based on one subject.

As I look back on how I discovered the various viewpoints among the people around me, I saw the color gray, meaning I realized the world was not black and white. Everyone looks at things differently and we should respect others' viewpoints. After all, each person has had different experiences or relationships that colored their perspective differently from yours.

I find great pride and Gratitude in how much I grew as a person when I was in college, simply because I learned to respect what others feel. I am not sure I could do many of the things today that bring me joy and satisfaction if I had not learned to respect others and their perspective. Despite there being a very disturbing political polarization in the USA today, I find I can talk to anyone, no matter what side of the issue they stand on. I choose to joke about any differences we may have or I'll make a joke about why don't we talk about something else, then I'll laugh and give them a friendly pat on the back. We are all created in G-d's Image and therefore we are all special and need to be treated with respect.

The transition period from childhood to young adulthood that I experienced at BU is one I am most deeply Grateful for. I had fun. I made some great friends. And I started to look at life in a more purposeful way.

BU was also the start of something that never got off the ground for me until nearly four decades later. It all started with a purchase of a television.

Chapter 9
THE AMAZING $69.99, PLUS TAX, TELEVISION

Growing up as a sports-loving youngster, I found the television to be a dear friend, even though back then the amount of games on TV were not nearly as plentiful as they are today. We didn't even get all the major games. A most grotesque example: I wasn't able to see the 1966-67 Philadelphia Seventy-Sixers championship-clinching game against the Warriors (nor their trumping of the hated Boston Celtics before that to lock up the Eastern division). Do kids today know how hard our lives were back then?

Aside from sports, I loved many TV programs like the hilarious *Three Stooges* shows that I could always count on being on. As with most families of the era, we had only one television. I often had to fight with my brother and sister over what to watch. How deprived was I? Only one TV for all three of us! How did we ever survive? On the plus side, I didn't have to deal with the parents wanting to monopolize it. My parents were not exactly lovers of the TV, or as they called it: the Boob Tube.

During my freshman year of college, I did not think much about TV. I was too busy discovering freedom. But my sophomore year was entirely different. My roommate and I decided one day that our floor needed a TV. I had some leftover cash and he had a borrowed car. That's all we needed to go find 12-inch black-and-white TV on sale for $69.99, plus tax.

We brought back my new purchase and immediately we became a social hub. Remember the saying *be careful for what you wish for*? Very soon every afternoon before dinner, that TV would be playing shows everyone, except me, just couldn't get enough of. While I loved having everyone over, I soon got bored watching. Eventually, a friend of mine next door invited me over to play cards. That was great fun, except he beat me at almost every game we played. The few I won were so rare that with each one, I felt as though I had climbed Mount Everest.

Looking back, I can see the irony: I discovered that I really did not need to watch TV around the clock like I thought I would only *after* I purchased my own television set. I didn't even need to watch it all day on Sundays even though, then, as is now in the U.S., Sundays are for watching NFL football. The line-up was simpler back then: there was one game on TV at one o'clock in the afternoon and another at four o'clock, neither of which had a pre-game show to whet your appetite.

As I think I made clear earlier, I am a football fan in general and a die-hard Eagles fan in particular. But after watching the first game on Sundays (which seldom featured my Eagles, who were awful the time) I found I had had enough and wanted to do something else. No one else shared my feelings. Unwilling to spend even more time inside losing card games, I found myself going out for walks and sometimes I'd find someone to throw a ball around with on a nice fall afternoon.

One Sunday, shortly after the first game was over, I was out walking alone when I saw a few runners pass me by. They were amazing. Every movement was in perfect harmony and they had bodies built to be perfect runners. Someone saw my amazement and told me the name of the group. They were training to contend to win the Boston Marathon.

I was inspired. Not too long after seeing those awesome athletes, I decided to try running. It was love at first step. Although I was not as disciplined and organized about my running as I am today, I did manage to get a run in one to two times each week. During the winter I cut back even further, but I took it up again in the spring.

On the third Monday of April in Boston, is the running of the most prestigious running event in the world. You need to qualify for it and the times are very difficult to say the least. Maybe when I am 100, if I am still running, I could qualify. Maybe not. But, since I was not training too hard, and I did not know about qualifying times, I began dreaming of the day I'd finish that race.

There are many who ask why we run. They point out that no one ever seems happy when they are running, only when they finish. Many people simply hate to run including accomplished athletes.

Runners will tell you they find joy and spiritual connection when running. It builds a sense of wellbeing and empowerment. Ask anyone who has ever finished a marathon or other long race and far more often than not, they will describe how it helped change their lives for the better. Running is also the most natural form of exercise. Just look at kids on the playground or at a park and you will see them running.

The running community is one of the most inclusive, encouraging and upbeat groups of people you will ever come across. I cannot tell you how many times I have been at the end of a race, struggling to finish when countless runners, who are many times faster than I and who had finished over an hour earlier, not only gave me encouragement but a look of respect that for me being out there so long. At the Odyssey Half Marathon in Philadelphia, which takes place a few minutes from my house, there is actually a beer garden by the finish line. Each runner gets a pint for free when they reach the end of the race. Beer and a half-marathon, no doubt cause all inhibitions to cease. I have always been so inspired by how everyone cheers for all finishers of that race, especially those last ones who are going at a very slow pace. We know how hard they are working and we want them to know they are very much one of us. Yes, there are finishers behind me! OK, I admit not too many.

For me, running was the first time in my life when I felt like I was an accomplished athlete. I learned very quickly that as long as you are running, you are a part of the sport. There is no team to make. You do not have to meet any time requirements to be considered a runner. When I ran, I felt as if I was playing a real sport, just like those runners I saw on that fateful Sunday in Boston. Then after a run, when I felt the endorphins kick in, I felt like a super star. My dreams of doing the Boston Marathon were stronger and stronger.

One of the great things I love about running, or any exercise for that matter, is that it can be an answer for whatever ails you in your world. Whether it's a tough class exam, trouble with lovers, money problems, or just about anything else that upsets you, going for a run will make you feel better. In my case, running helped me forget about how disappointed I was in all my Philadelphia teems.

During my BU days from 1969 to 1973, Philadelphia teams were truly pathetic. To make matters worse, I was around New Yorkers and Bostonians who had at least one, and often more teams to brag about. While the Flyers (NHL Hockey) in my senior year became an up-and-coming team, every other Philly team was eliminated from post season action about one-third of the way through the exhibition season. The worst case had to be the Flyers, who were stopped one year from making the playoffs when a goal was scored by the other team with just four seconds left in the final game. Four seconds from the playoffs! I can still hear friends saying, "The Flyers are going to make the playoffs! Oops! A goal was scored with 4 seconds left. Bye-bye playoffs. Sorry, Roy." Yeah, they were sorry! After that rather traumatic incident, I remember having one great run. It was my answer. It made the crushing loss not so bad.

You are probably wondering why I am so devoted to Philly teams who constantly fail to win championships. The answer is simple: I love Philadelphia and its surrounding areas, including the Jersey Shore. While it is agony to see them all lose, I admit I enjoy the misery-loves-company camaraderie with my fellow Philly fans.

Interestingly, many years later I learned some great lessons about being a sports fan from the Pittsburgh Steelers and New York Yankees. For those of you who hate the Steelers and Yankees, please bear with me. Both those teams have won more titles than any other team in their respective sport. Yet as I write this, the Steelers have not won the Super Bowl around 90% of the time, and the Yankees lost about 75%. Remember: they are the best. There is a message in that. Those numbers tell us that even the best lose most of the time. So, before you get too wrapped up in your teams, remember those numbers to avoid being depressed because you don't have a championship to brag about.

But back to running. During college, I also used running to help me get through the stress of finals and to help me write some papers. After a run, I became calmer and better able to focus on studying.

Often during a run, I would come up with an idea that would help me write a paper. A couple of times I had been intimidated by the subject for a tough final but then I'd go for a run and suddenly I had the confidence to take it on. If I could run, my thought was, I could attack the final and not be so scared.

Another gift running gave me was, for the first time in my life, I was part of a sport. A few of my fraternity brothers were also into running. It was really neat to compare notes with them, especially since they were significantly better than I was. But I didn't care. The early 70s was the dawn of a running boom and I was a part of it. With every article or news story, I could feel the energy and joy of being a true athlete. They were talking about me! The problem for me was that although the sport was catching on, it was nothing like today. Now, virtually every weekend day and some week nights in warm weather, you can find a race. Even during colder months there are very few, if any, weekends when at least one race isn't run. If I had been able to find a race back then, it would have been one uplifting experience for me. Knowing what I know about them now, I would have felt such a triumph after so many years of being a failure at sports. But, as I would find out later in life, not racing was a Blessing in disguise.

My passion for running, as strong as it was, could not be called consistent. When it would rain or snow as it frequently does in Boston in the winter, I would take a hiatus for a couple weeks or more. At the time there were no treadmills or indoor tracks to run on. Plus, I admit I was a relatively carefree college student who went from activity to activity not exactly focused enough to do anything really well, and that included running. Oftentimes I would even forgo it to play other sports like flag football, basketball or softball. I even tried playing floor hockey, which lasted for only one shift. The ball came to me, just ten feet in front of the net. I was ready to shoot, score and raise my stick and arms in celebration. Only I missed completely and hit an opponent on the face who also happened to be a friend of mine. As a humanitarian I decided not to take another shift. The sport was definitely better without me.

In a memorable basketball game, we played a team made up of players who had just missed making the junior varsity at BU. While

BU was not, nor is, a basketball powerhouse, being close is still pretty impressive. For some reason, I decided to just shoot when I came in, as we were down by something like 30 points after five minutes. It was my night. I hit something like five shots in a row, and although we were still down by a bunch, I was the hero for our team. That was the first half. In the second half I received a true sign of respect: I was double teamed by our opposition. I never got a shot off and we lost by 40 or whatever.

The crazy thing is, my smartest night in sports at BU actually happened in a football game. There were two linemen on each side of the ball who would block or rush the passer or try to stop a running play. A close friend of mine and I were supposed to split offense and defense for each half. I drew offense for the first half. On the first play my opponent tried to take my head off with a forearm. I recognized him as someone who had been kicked off the BU team for being crazy, or as we called it *psychotic*. I was ready for him the next play. We were going to lose anyway so I was intent only on making sure I would not lose life or limb. He blew by me without any resistance from me and recorded a sack. My teammates told me to block him and I said: "you block him."

No one had a problem with my response except for my close friend. I pleaded with him not to block the guy in the second half. I begged him to save himself. We were already losing by a ridiculous amount anyway. Sadly he tried valiantly, and ended up on the carpet on the first play with a dislocated foot that you could diagnose without a doctor. Our psychotic opponent showed great compassion complaining, "Let's get the game going." We laugh about it to this day.

Another memorable night was a softball game where I was drafted to pitch. It was slow pitch, meaning you had to have an arc on the ball. No one told me that and I pitched semi-fast. No one complained. It was a close game and I was turning into a hero. That is until in the last inning. A teammate misjudged a hit that should have been the final out and that, instead, went for a game-winning two-run homerun. During the next game, the umpire was versed in the rules and I was taken out quickly after surrendering something like five or six homeruns.

By the time my tenure at BU was ending in the spring of 1973, I started to think about my athletic situation in a different way. As we heard stories about what life was like in the working world, one thing was very clear: we could no longer count on being able to find sports to play all the time, like in college. Sure your weekends would be without worry over studying (actually that was not too much of a worry for me) but the work world would be very busy for everyone. No longer could you go out and throw a ball around or shoot baskets in the middle of the day. Running could even be a challenge. Sure you just run, but what would happen if you are working twelve-hour days and then driving back and forth from home? Intramurals were great in college but no one talked about work intramurals.

I knew there would be a great challenge for me. But as I faced the challenge, I could not help but reflect on my athletic failures as a youth.

The running and other sports at BU were different than what I experienced in my youth. In college I played on some teams without great humiliation and discovered a sport where I finally felt accomplished. Meanwhile, I recognized that there were many guys who were successful athletes in their youth only to feel letdown after college (I stress that not *all* triumphant high-school athletes feel that way). I became determined that after BU, I would use my love of running to keep me in shape and look upon myself as a successful athlete. Though at the time, I did not realize that my struggles as a young kid would actually become the foundation of unimaginable success.

It is said that G-d works in funny ways. As I will be describing my amazing accomplishments athletically, I am Grateful for the Almighty watching over me. I am so Grateful for what I can do.

That Gratitude does not stop with me. When I see others finish a race and give that smile that says *this will change my life*, I am so Grateful to watch them and feel their joy. I call them "my people." They are where I came from. I will never forget that once I was a loser at sports, who has turned it around.

One final word about exercise and fitness: According to the

common calendar, a new year begins on January 1 and there is a lot of hype about New Year's resolutions. Here's a vital piece of advice: never ever make New Year's resolutions. Typically, people make a lot of them and fail after just a couple weeks or so. The proof can be found at fitness facilities, which starting January 1 become ridiculously overcrowded only to become normal again when the New Year's resolution folks drop out usually by February.

Instead, I suggest you perpetually keep making resolutions; don't just make them on New Year's Day. If you fail, keep trying and at least get part of it right. When it comes to measuring your fitness, that might mean just working out one day per week. It may mean just walking a couple days a week. Just do not give up. Always adjust so you will enjoy your work outs whatever they are in order that you will keep coming back. You might have to regroup and figure out what exercise works best for you as well as what timing and venue. This approach is actually something that can work for everything you want to improve in your life.

Chapter 10
THE HANDSHAKE WAKES ME UP

In January of 1974, Gail and I had friends over to play some games. I was living alone at the time and Gail was living at home. My housecleaning, as Gail would say, left more than a lot to be desired. Mine was the typical bachelor abode as my mother's doctor neatly summed up recently when telling us he had a new girlfriend. My mother asked where they would live and he answered his place. Then he added quite humorously that some changes would be made to his place because "what woman likes the décor of a man who has been living alone in happy bachelorhood?"

That night everything went wrong. The friends were sets of couples who were fighting over something and took it out by trying to beat each other at whatever unimportant game we were playing. Gail and I tried to joke about it as a way to defuse it, but to no avail. The night's lowest point came when they asked for coffee. Then, as now, I do not drink coffee. But I was OK with making instant coffee that I had purchased for them. Who knew about cream and sugar or sugar substitute? I didn't, but no problem. I had milk I used for cereal. Only the milk was old. It curdled in the coffee.

The night with the friends ended. Gail and I looked at each other and, after they were far enough away, we let out a big laugh. We talked about the evening until I asked her to marry me. She said, "What?" And then we embraced. She never did say *yes,* but after 41-plus years of a wonderful marriage, I guess I got my answer.

We decided to wait until we both finished school to tie the knot. The time leading up to our marriage was far from blissful. Her father's brain tumor was spreading. It was clear that he was dying. Sadly, he passed before we got married. What is profoundly sad, though, is that he has missed so much joy that we could have brought to him. His memory has certainly been for a Blessing.

As the summer approached, I started to notice that my inconsistency in running and working out could cause me to fall back into becoming a loser athletically, as in my earlier life. I wrestled with how to motivate myself throughout the season and came up with a plan by late summer. I realized a sports series such as basketball, baseball and hockey had seven games just like the week. I decided to play a series every week. If I exercised, I won that day, and vice versa. If I didn't manage to exercise, I lost. To spice things up, I challenged myself to my own "championship." At the end of my first year, I would have to run approximately 3.9 miles from my apartment to Gail's house. While the plan made a lot of sense, I was not totally sold that I could pull it off.

And of course, I'd have to begin it before I could finish it.

That beginning was jump started by a fortuitous handshake from Gail's father. I had discovered a way to shake hands with someone far stronger than me and not feel the pain should he try to press me into submission. By late August, Gail's father had very little strength but he told me to try my handshake defense on him. He crushed my hand in an instant. We both laughed with him laughing much more than me. When I got home that night, I looked in the mirror and told myself that if he could do that in his condition, I could start my program. I decided to start my year on Rosh Hashanah, the Jewish New Year that takes place early fall.

The first week I found myself down 2 to 4 before I realized what was going on. Then I made it 3 to 4 and was mad at myself for not planning better. I have never lost another week since, unless it involved sickness or injury. In October 2012, I suffered a concussion on a training run when an out-of-control bike hit me and knocked my head to the ground. I lost that week 0-7, effectively stopping my 9½-year streak of never losing a week. It was also the only week I failed to win at least one day. I went on a winning streak of 16 weeks

71

before back spasms from tennis caused me to lose again. During that streak I became hooked on my league-competition-sport, whatever you want to call it. Today I typically win around 95-99% of my days. Doing at least some form of exercise is the foundation of my endurance sports success that I enjoy today.

At first I admit I was a little timid about talking about this. I had invented my own way to be a champion without any competition or anyone even knowing about it except for Gail. Gail, as usual was very supportive and would ask me if I won my day before making plans. In actuality I did have a lot of competition. There was, first of all myself. I had to overcome inertia to get a work out. The other forms of competition involved work and other commitments.

Traveling during those early years was very difficult as I would go from early morning until after dinner. Dinner often consisted of heavy food and drink and I would not get back until late at night. Also, at that time, I did not have as many ways to get my exercise in. Today I have core exercises and walking to get in my work out at any place and any time.

Keeping me going in those early years were many who were very impressed with my diligence and consistency. On New Years' I have very mixed emotions about what happens at fitness facilities. As they advertise for people to get in shape, I am proud that means nothing related to me. At the same time, I am sad that so many people do not know how good it feels to be in shape and how much joy it can bring to you. I also feel the pain of friends who go to fitness facilities that are overrun in January and February, the weeks you really do need an indoor facility, with the New Year's resolution crowd.

As that first year progressed, I increasingly became excited about doing what I called "The Run." The funny thing is that today I can run or walk 3.9 miles and consider it nothing more than a work out. But back then, it was like climbing Mt. Everest. I decided on Monday, May 19, 1975, to try The Run. I choose May 19 because it was the anniversary of The Flyers first Stanley Cup. I put on a Flyers shirt and headed out. Unfortunately, I was too excited and went out way too fast. And when someone beeped at me for the Flyers shirt, I decided it was not my day. I went back home to lick my wounds. That day I learned an important lesson when doing any run: never go

72

out too fast or get too excited; stay calm and pace yourself.

The next day, May 20, I woke up relaxed. My wedding to Gail was just five days away and our two-month honeymoon to Europe and Israel was less than two weeks away. I had breakfast and did whatever I needed to do. Late in the afternoon I got the feeling that *this* would be my day to do The Run. So I started out, going very slowly and relaxed.

I had a lot to be Grateful for and happy about, so I told myself to just enjoy the run wherever it takes you. I passed where I had stopped the day before and realized I felt great. I thought about the point of no return, where I would be halfway there. I reached that point and realized I had a real chance to succeed. Then I saw a major intersection in Philadelphia: Haverford and City Line. Once I made a left turn there, it was a short distance. I waited for a car to let me go then I started to celebrate. I raised my hands and let out victory yell along with a huge smile. I told myself to calm down not celebrate too soon. There were a few more blocks and then I'd be home free. A little over a month before I turned 24, I finally had a "championship." My first year in my new system of exercise had ended in a complete success!

The question then was: *what do I do now?* I was dressed in running clothes without money and without even an ID (this is before 9/11). I knocked on Gail's door and raised my hands in the air in triumph, but with a little trepidation. Gail had wonderful relatives from Australia staying with her. How would they react to find the groom all sweaty and in clothing that's not exactly what one likes to see others wear when they sit down to dinner? Gail was again the best. She told me she would drive me home but first I needed to eat. What a great dinner it was. Once again, I found out what a fantastic woman I was about to marry.

Since everyone, including me was thinking about the wedding, my triumph quickly went to the back of my mind as well as everyone else's. Actually, I'm not sure any even gave it more than a passing thought. But in the intervening years of personal athletic success between then and now, I have put that accomplishment in perspective. Before that year, I was someone who wanted to have success as an athlete. My youth had been a total failure. In college I flirted with taking my personal sports to a new level, but never got around to it. But that year I found something that worked for me.

By virtue of that system working for me and the years to this day, it was a stroke of genius on my part. I am deeply Grateful for that fateful handshake and what it led me to start. We are all motivated by different things and we never know what will work until we try it.

As I will soon describe, my running would take a long, frustrating road to future success. What I accomplished that year, with that run, is no different than what makes other people successful runners or endurance athletes in general. Everything is based upon what your personal goals are and how you accomplish them. One of my favorite sayings about running races is that we do not race to race against each other, but race to be with each other. The term PR (personal record) is something that everyone can relate to. Congratulate yourself when you accomplish it. I am always so touched when I tell a much faster runner of my PR and hear them congratulate me with sincerity, even though theirs is many times faster than mine.

Part of the joy of May 20, 1975, was no doubt the fact I had never enjoyed true athletic success. That day, for the first time in my life, in the back of my mind I started to be Grateful for all my failures as a youth. Success felt so great at that moment. Had I enjoyed stardom as a youngster running 3.9 miles would not have meant so much. But on that day, it was everything as well as the start of great pleasure in my life. Not only did I soon afterward marry Gail, but the Flyers won their second straight Stanley Cup a week to the day later, the only back-to-back championship any of my teams have ever enjoyed in my lifetime.

As it turns out, my way of keeping track of my athletic progress is really not so crazy. Many elite athletes carefully track their progress and feel the motivation, if not pressure, to get work outs in. What I learned with charting my athletics that year was that it helps to have two vital things going for you when you start something new. First you need a measuring method to know how you are doing. In the real estate business, that would be how many and for how much were the deals you closed in a given time. For teachers, it could mean students test scores. For losing weight, it would mean what do you weigh along with what events or holidays did you have to get through.

The second help is motivation. In my case it was Gail's father's handshake telling me I've had enough excuses and procrastination. For an athlete doing a race, it could mean honoring a loved one when you do the race, as many do with cancer events. It could mean redemption in the case of doing a long-distance, organized bike ride that you failed to finish due to mechanical problems or a cramp. For someone recovering from an addiction, it could be a photo of your loved ones you have become estranged from. Whatever it is for you, find it. In it you will also find the Gratitude for the chance to follow through on goals.

Chapter 11
IRISH TWINS

After a wonderful two-month honeymoon with Gail—actually with Gail every day is a honeymoon, though I can see her rolling her eyes and saying "speak for yourself" with a huge laugh from me—I entered the family business, making me the third generation. The job was supposed to last forever. There was supposed to be enough money to support us forever.

At the time I felt very lucky and I wanted to prove I deserved all the good fortune. For the first couple of years, I was sent to our corrugated box plant. Then after a year or so, we opened a caulking cartridge plant in Ohio. We needed sales to support this investment so I was sent to Dayton, Ohio to bring in some sales staff to support our new facility. Some explanation is needed to describe what we had to offer. We made a paper cartridge with a plastic spout that companies who made adhesives used to package their product. We did not make the adhesive and we were out of the business before plastic cartridges took over the industry.

The year or so Gail and I lived in Ohio was difficult. The town was based around kids and at that time; we were childless and very content for the moment to remain so. It did offer us the chance to explore on weekends. We spent about half our weekends in somewhere other than Dayton. Cincinnati was our most frequent destination. We grew to enjoy the town as it was far more of a city than Dayton. When we moved to Ohio we were had been living in center city Philadelphia, and loved what cities have to offer. Dayton's downtown was miniscule. One very positive thing that did come out

76

of Dayton: we are both so happy to live in the Philadelphia area again. We live in Merion and formerly lived in Center City Philadelphia. We also have a place in Ventnor, NJ. I love these places and am deeply Grateful for them and the joy they bring me every day.

Gail was very supportive of me, and that was vital to my business success out there. She worked teaching special education to autistic kids. To make matters worse for her, I was away about half the time. When I was not away, it was just the two of us. That was never a problem for us. We know how to give each other plenty of space. For instance, Gail loves to take long leisurely walks. I am more than happy to let her go and she is very happy I do my many endurance events.

Perhaps the most memorable time in Dayton was when there was an historical blizzard in late January, 1978. It started Wednesday night and shut everything down until Monday morning. Our apartment did not lose water or electricity, so we could watch TV in comfort. At the time that was all that was available. Imagine no computer or ordering movies. Long-distance telephone was also not cheap like today. Although neither of us then, or now, are big drinkers we had happy hour earlier and earlier during that four-day period.

Despite a not too robust social, or any other type of life, in Dayton, our time there was very important for me. I took to sales right away. I called countless companies via telephone looking for business. For a couple of places where we knew several caulking manufacturers were located, I'd fly out and call upon them in person. I would regularly call on places like Atlanta, St. Louis, Kansas City, Dallas, parts of Ohio and Indiana. One trip had me leaving at four o'clock in the morning on a plane from Dayton to Atlanta for breakfast, followed by a flight to New Orleans for lunch, and ending with a flight to Dallas for dinner. You probably could not do that today. After a couple of times, I stopped doing that rather insane trip. I travelled so much, there were times that I would forget where I was. I would always laugh to myself when someone working at a hotel would tell me, in a very matter-of-fact tone, where I was. Such is life on the road.

No doubt the most memorable trip was to Kansas City to see a good customer shortly after New Year's. Typically, we would go to a bar for a few beers and some dinner before I would go to my hotel room where I'd wake up the next day for a flight to St. Louis. On that fateful night, we went to a new bar in Kansas City, Kansas. It wasn't really a bar. Back then bars were not permitted in Kansas (I'm not sure of the law today.) You were, however, allowed to have "private clubs" that were "very" restrictive: you needed a dollar to join.

Being a young salesman who looked younger than his age, I made it a point to wear a suit all the time to look professional. On that night I was wearing an impeccable three-piece suit that looked more expensive than it was. We walked into the bar that, if you described it as seedy it would have be an upgrade for what it was. I was, with my dapper suit, immediately made to feel like a target for a robbery or worse.

We sat at the bar and things got even more threatening for me. My customer had won a small fortune on betting at the college bowl games and wanted to repay me for all the times I treated for beer and dinner. He rolled out his wad of $100 bills and motioned for a stripper to come over and take care of me.

I have always taken my marriage to Gail very seriously and wanted no part of the action. Though at the time, I was not worried about that as much as the look the rather ornery men were giving me. Their faces clearly told me: "Please go up there. You look like you have a mint and we want your money." My customer was rather drunk and oblivious of all of that. As I always did, I knew how to hold my liquor. I would usually have just two or three sips of beer and then let the rest get warm. That way, I would order another cold one to "keep up" while sending the unfinished one back to be put down the drain. But that night, I was so nervous I gulped too many and was also drunk.

It is said that selling brings out your plan-B ability or improvisation when your original plan goes awry. I instinctively went to the bathroom and came out holding my stomach complaining of an awful stomach ache. Fortunately, my customer was too drunk to realize it was an act and was at the point where he was enjoying himself too much to really notice. Of course, I prefer to think I was just such a great actor that night. I caught a glimpse of the other patrons who were very disappointed I was leaving with my fortune, but I was not about to hang around and console them.

Since this was more than 35 years ago I guess I can write that I broke the law on drunk driving that night. Not knowing how to drive drunk, I screamed to myself every command to drive without causing an accident. Since I wanted to be done with that night, I went to the airport grabbed a late-night flight, canceled my hotel in Kansas City and booked one in St. Louis.

But my troubles that night were not over, and the new troubles were nothing compared to what I faced in the bar. The flight attendant told me I needed coffee and I was totally dependent upon her good judgment. I drank two cups of coffee, more than I had had in the aggregate for the past twelve months. I was up all night, but safe in my hotel room in St. Louis. I was able to sleep it off a little the next morning as my appointments didn't begin until nine and there was an hour time zone difference.

It is with great regret that the postmortem on that evening was the last conversation I had with my customer. I called him about three weeks later to see how he was and naturally could not help but to ask how his new hang out was. To my shock, he told me he would never go there again. At first I thought *Great! You came to your senses. But why did you have to subject me to that place?* He continued before I could say anything though and told me one the ladies of the night working there went out with a John who was found the next day, stabbed to death. I had no idea how to answer him other than to say how horrible that was. He told me to call him in a couple of weeks for an order. We would never speak again. When I made the call, someone else had taken over his job. He was fired for stealing.

Fortunately for me, that was a very isolated incident. I truly enjoyed calling on everyone I called on. When we decided that a couple accounts were too small to pursue, I found it very difficult to tell the folks I had gotten to know that we would no longer be pursuing them. Despite any anger about the business decision, in all cases they wished me well.

South Bend, Indiana is the home of Notre Dame University, called

The Fighting Irish for their sports teams. Of course their biggest sport is football. At present they command their own television deal unlike any other football program. Being a sports fan, I was thrilled to go to South Bend on business to try to break, or land, a major account with Uniroyal (a big company at the time). My first meeting went very well and I could tell sooner or later, I would be doing a lot of business with them. The meeting was in the morning. After which, I decided to make some calls (payphone only in the 70s) and then grab some lunch. The lunch was fine but the dessert was even better. For the heck of it, I looked at the yellow pages under adhesives and found a company about a mile away.

On the way home I decided to stop by and cold call them. It has been said that timing is everything. That day my timing was perfect. The owner happened to have had a problem with his present caulking cartridge supplier. His was a growing company so he was open to opportunities. He told me to come into his office right away. He was fascinated by both our company and me.

Having the same last name as the company, meant I was an owner. That wasn't actually correct but it wasn't important at the time. What was important, is that he was an entrepreneur who had started his business several years prior. We hit it off right away. Both his business and mine were smaller companies that had found success by running circles around our bigger competition. I described the philosophy at our composite can and tube plant of doing anything to get a delivery in time to our customer, no matter how last-minute the request was. When I told him our new delivery turnaround was made possible by our new manufacturing plant, his eyes lit up.

This may sound easy but it took a lot of follow-up to do business with him. He had to provide us with new labels and could not just make a fast change since he was on the hook for a lot of labels with his soon-to-be-former supplier. But the opportunity was a great way for me to show him my persistence. One thing most people do not realize is that persistence is probably the most important part of success in sales.

As time went by our mutual admiration for each other grew. I was very impressed with him for starting a business from ground zero and he loved my young energy and the fact that I was trying to contribute to the family business not just inherit it. I actually moved back to Philadelphia before the account broke but I know he mentioned me numerous times to my father and the salesman who took over for me. He remains one of my favorite people in my business life.

Uniroyal did break for us during my tenure in Ohio and grew rapidly for us a couple years later. I called these accounts my Irish Twins and am forever in their debt. At age 27 I had finally made my mark on the family business. It felt great. In later years, when the family business liquidated, my early success there reminded me that I knew that selling was for me.

Upon coming back to Philadelphia, I began selling folding cartons for our company. It was with a major account that I now present to you what a salesperson has to go through to make a sale.

After months of trying to break into a household-named account in Baltimore, I finally got a trial run. The order was small, but the upside was huge. If we could perform, no doubt more would follow. Upon receiving the order, I was instructed to work with their quality control department. The man assigned seemed like a nice guy, so I looked forward to having lunch with him on my first visit.

As any salesperson will tell you, you should always find out your clients' interests and talk to them about it to ingratiate yourself to your customer. This is sales 101. The problem for me was this guy only cared to talk about one thing and one thing only: his eleven-year-old son's basketball team where he was one of the assistant coaches. We would talk for close to two hours about the team and all the players, along with every practice and game. I would have to listen to him express his dissatisfaction with referees and yes, it got more than a little colorful. For the heck of it, once I changed the subject and saw him drift away from me. Laughing to myself, I asked another question about the team.

It was so bad, I had to take notes on each kid and extra notes on his son. His eyes would light up when I would ask if, say, his son scored his whatever-number point of the season. We would always have lunch in the same place with very small distance between tables.

81

One day after lunch and another appointment, I went to make calls at a payphone. Before I could reach the phone, a stranger came up to me and told me how impressed he was that I could listen to all I had to listen to at lunch. I recognized him as the man who had sat at the table next to us. After a great laugh, I thanked him for the compliment. It is truly amazing how a compliment from a stranger can make you feel great.

In spite of my efforts, we never made much of the account due to the fact they were bought out shortly thereafter. All that listening and studying a team of kids I would never meet, were for naught.

There was one account I never did break into. The company had a very unusual arrangement. They were famously successful and located in the northeast corner of Pennsylvania. The owners were from central New York State. They would come down on Monday morning and leave on Thursday night to go back to their families. The women who worked as secretaries were breathtaking. The rumors about what went on there were mindboggling.

And then there was the account where the guy we did business with would often brag about how much partying and drinking he did. Just before New Year's Eve, I asked him about his plans for the big night, expecting a great story. He looked slightly insulted and said he goes to bed at ten o'clock that evening so he could get up early and visit friends and relatives. He called it "amateur night." He told me how sickening he found it that all those idiots who did not know how to drink thought they could have such a good time that they could make up for a boring year in one night.

I did break a major account in the Baltimore area. The company made paper products and needed a specialized box that we happened to specialize. In addition to bringing us great business, my contact was genuinely a great guy. I very much enjoyed my sales calls with him. We even kept in touch for a couple years after I stopped calling on him because our company made the decision to get out of that business.

The decision had nothing to do with me. Many manufactures were moving out of the northeast, including out of Philadelphia, to go south or overseas. Not much was replacing those companies. That meant that business essentially was leaving the area because you could not expect to compete with freight costs amidst a very competitive industry. Folding carton companies were not leaving so the same numbers of companies were fighting for less of a pie.

This phase of my business life was very important for three reasons. The first was that I found what my father called self-worth. I was successful because of my efforts, not because of what I was born into. My Irish Twins were not buying from me because my last name was Kardon, they were buying from me because I was Roy. My paper products accounts bought from *me*, not from the company as my client had told me once. He said something to the effect that I was a hustler who was honest and straight forward. The company in South Bend that I had called on from the phone book was always impressed with my follow through. Uniroyal appreciated how I would work with them.

During that time, I remember, getting psyched up for my sales calls and trips. I would constantly be thinking about how I could do better all the time, even during non-business hours. For the first time in life, I felt a swagger about what I was doing. Swagger, when used properly, indicates confidence in yourself, and for the first time in my life, that's what I had. In many ways, that era was my coming of age.

The second reason the selling phase in my life was important is because of it, I found my profession. Today I am a commercial real estate broker, as I will cover in "Always Losing, Always Hopeful." When the family business would run its course, I knew I could always sell. It is who I am and I am proud of that. It is said that the best salespeople are former athletes. In my case it is *present* athlete. The reason is *not* that athletes are used to winning, it is that they are used to bouncing back after losing. I love that fact about sales because it gives me one of the keys to happiness: resilience. It is a great antidote for depression.

The third reason that era is important to me is that through the sales aspect of it, I discovered that I genuinely like people. Yes, I know there are many who are mean and evil out there. There are many selfish people who do not care about anything but themselves. There are also violent people, etc. And there are far too many periods of time when it seems nations become evil on the whole such as with Nazi Germany or ISIS today. But despite all that, I find myself very blessed to genuinely enjoy meeting people, even if for only a moment. In "Joy Amidst the Sadness" I will describe my many meetings with patients and their families in hospital situations, and how I look upon myself as the one who benefits more from those visits as a volunteer Chaplain. Please do not think of this as totally altruistic. It is a far better way to live and much easier life when you find happiness in the world because you think there is something very special and wonderful about everyone you meet.

Selling also offers you many reasons to be Grateful. In my experience from my various sales positions, I have found sales people are always pursuing a sale in one form or another. There is always, as I will go into detail in "Always Losing, Always Hopeful," an account, customer, deal, etc. that you are going after to get you excited. You also are never doing the same thing every day. There are different people, companies, opportunities, venues, etc. to keep you invigorated. The job, career, and profession that will work for you, is one where the mundane repetitive tasks are something you like. Many people want to sit at a desk and work the computer, phone, etc. Others want to work outdoors and with their hands. Finding what is right for you is key to being happy. Always ask yourself, *is this what I want to do every day?* I pray for your success, not just monetarily but in being satisfied with your work life.

During this period I was not praying every day but I did keep Kosher, both inside and outside the home. Somehow I managed to do it at that time. On the road it was virtually impossible to find kosher meat or poultry, so I found myself eating fish or vegetarian meals before it became at all fashionable to be vegetarian. On the rare times I had an issue, my customers were great about it and would go to another place or would understand why I was only eating a salad and baked potato. What keeping Kosher gave me was a way to keep connected to the Almighty. With every bite of food, I was reminded of Him.

I am forever Grateful for this period of my life. It marked the beginning of me becoming the man I am today. It is when I came of age in so many ways.

Chapter 12
How Dare You Take My Time
Asking Me a Question?

As I mentioned, upon returning from our honeymoon, I went to work at our corrugated box plant. I quickly got into rhythm of work and exercising. I continued to enjoy running and while I had not yet found my natural passion in business selling, work was coming along.

At first, I worked in personnel where I made frequent trips to the plant, which meant I went up and down stairs as the office was on the second floor. To get to our plant manager's office, I needed to go up five steps.

One day those steps started me on a journey that would, in some ways, make my athletic failures as a youth totally unimportant, as if they never existed. It would drive me to many publically embarrassing moments and challenge all the accomplishments I enjoyed the year before when I made that magical run. Decades later, those troubles would be the foundation for me giving myself my middle name, Attitude of Gratitude. It did and does continue to bring tears of Gratitude to me.

The day was a normal day with nothing memorable or all that important. As I was going up to see the plant manager on the steps, I felt a pain in my knee that felt ominous. I had never before experienced any pain in the knee before and thought there must be something wrong. Accordingly, I went to a sports medicine specialist whose name will go unmentioned except to say I have a friend today who shared the same experience with this doctor. At the time, this doctor was all over the place in terms of being a team doctor to both colleges and professional organizations in Philadelphia. The doctor was also on the news a few times as his reputation was very renowned.

I called for an appointment and found the wait to see this doctor was several weeks. While I was not happy about the wait, I took the appointment anyway. I was able in that time to do some non-running related workouts to keep in shape and keep winning my weeks. But I was very nervous about my situation. I had waited all my life to find athletic success and now it was being threatened of being taken away from me. Since my knowledge at the time was miniscule, I worried about my entire athletic future.

Our plant was located about fifteen or twenty miles away from the doctor's office and it was a bit of a problem getting there, but I arrived on time, ready to save my running career. I walked into the office and said to myself, "this is not good." There were numerous people waiting ahead of me and the staff was, to say the least, not exactly welcoming.

I sat for about two hours past my appointment time. When the staff called my name, I was nervous and very insecure about this whole experience. Another fifteen minutes in an exam room and the almighty doctor walked in. The doctor examined me for maybe two minutes and then in a Marine drill sergeant's voice barked out orders to me to move around. He curtly told me the procedure for strengthening without saying why or what my prognosis was.

Then I did the unthinkable. I asked him a question about when I could run again. The almighty doctor looked at me with a nasty expression and walked away with an angry face that said, *How dare you take my time with that question? You are not important enough to ask me anything!* One the assistants or students told me whenever I felt up to it, but watch for the pain.

My condition was runner's knee. Today it is easily treated with far more convenient and effective strategies than was around in the mid-1970s. The almighty doctor gave me instructions with leg lifts that included buying all this cumbersome equipment. To further add to my misery it was difficult to find anywhere in our apartment to set it up.

Subsequent to that episode that would last for a while, I learned easier ways and even found another doctor and physical therapist who explained what runner's knee is all about and the principle of strengthening that has, today, eradicated the condition for me.

In 2011, I had a reoccurrence of runner's knee due to a 10K race I did that involved a lot of downhill running. It caused me pain on a training run but to my surprise, my sports medicine doctor very nonchalantly told me I could have run for several miles with the pain. A couple years later, I discovered on my own how to do about three minutes of strengthening exercises that have since solved my problem of runner's knee.

However, let's get back to my experience with the almighty doctor that would last for about five years. I carefully followed the plans to get back to running. After two or three weeks, I was ready to try again. My first run or two were not long but were pain free. I was back, so I thought. But on the third, the pain returned. I decided not to go back to the almighty doctor. Instead, I concentrated on other exercises that were OK, but not particularly enjoyable as running was.

Eventually, I returned to the almighty doctor who again kept me waiting and was annoyed to even see me again. His attitude this time was: *I told you what your problem is now leave me alone.* In addition to being a very frustrating and demeaning experience, the time I took off from work was significant.

The problems I had to overcome would not be around today. There are numerous sports medicine doctors today who will set an appointment according to you being a patient, not an annoyance like the way the almighty doctor treated people. They generally care about you unlike the bad doctor who "treated" me in the 1970s. In addition to doctors, there are also physical therapists out there who will explain what you need to do and will actually take the time to work with you so you can get back to your passion. There is also equipment out there you can buy for your home or you can join a fitness center.

My experience with this callous doctor lasted about five years. I kept trying, only to feel pain that would keep me from running. I remember running in Rittenhouse Square in Philadelphia where we lived and feeling pain at the start of my run. It also felt like everyone was looking at me; like I was the biggest loser of all time. Although I knew this was far from the case, it still hurt. I had heard you should not run on the concrete of Rittenhouse Square so I tried Franklin Field at the University of Pennsylvania.

I love Franklin field. It is the venue where I started going to Philadelphia Eagles' games. My sister was a cheerleader of Penn just a couple of years before. Franklin Field is the oldest college football stadium still in use. The first scoreboard for a college football stadium was there and the first commercial television broadcast took place there. It was thought that the first radio broadcast was there, too, but it wound up being preempted by another one about a year before. For more than 100 years, the largest track and field event has taken place there. The best event ever: the Eagles beating the Packers on December 26, 1960 to win their last NFL championship, happened there. I went there eager to prove my athleticism on hallowed ground.

I wasn't alone. There were many other athletes around. They all looked far more accomplished than I was. On my first lap, the pain came back. I had to leave, humiliated. Again no one noticed but to me the whole stadium was booing me. I had failed on sacred ground to be a runner.

Although I would fail to get back into running at that time, I did not give up easily. I read everything I could (unfortunately this was before the advent of the internet and Google) trying to find a way to run. I talked to everyone I could about how to overcome the problem. I wanted so desperately to run.

Finally, I came upon orthotics as a way to get me back to the road, running. Orthotics are a shoe implant you use to improve your step so your body is aligned the way it should be to prevent all sorts of bad stuff. To get one you need to go to a podiatrist. I discovered one with the same reputation as the almighty doctor, but without the attitude. The podiatrist made me an orthotic I used for years. Unfortunately, it did not totally solve my knee problems and I developed Achilles tendon issues the orthotic could not help.

About five years after I first felt the pain I thought I would just do a 5K (3.1 miles) to experience the joy of finishing a race. I did everything imaginable to get to the starting line. I did those cumbersome exercises to strengthen my quads and work up gradually to doing the race. I was up to about two miles with no major pain and felt this would be my time. Then on a dreary Monday I had to walk up some stairs only to experience the knee pain the day after my Achilles tendon again acted up on a run. I threw in the towel, so to speak and did not get to the finish line. My running career was over, or so I thought.

This period in my life is something I never really was bitter or angry over. As I will describe in the next chapter, "Resilience Leads to Excellence," the joy of keeping myself in shape, along with the exhilaration of doing something special like my May 20, 1975, 3.9 mile run, gave me enough taste of winning that, to this day, I have never let it go. Nor do I have any intention of releasing. For my health to give me the chance to do it all, is something I am deeply Grateful for.

My Gratitude extends to living in the awesome country of the USA, where anyone can train and do various forms of athletic accomplishments. Shortly after the horrific tragic Boston Marathon bombing in that wonderful city, there was a North Korean Marathon. There is no way that repressive government would let any North Korean run unless they had a legitimate shot at winning and thereby bringing glory to that country's despotic leadership. I am so Grateful for the human spirit that I have, that I can make a decision to keep trying, never give up and eventually succeed.

The frustration I felt from the almighty doctor is also something that in hindsight I feel very Blessed to have experienced. No, I am not a masochist and definitely did not feel fortunate in any way while the almighty doctor was treating me. But that experience has made me a very determined athlete who networks, researches and does anything to get back to exercising whenever anything stands in my way. In today's world there are so many obstacles to staying in shape. Work life is hectic and always taking up a lot of time. I have an awful commute that every day takes about one hour and forty-five minutes unless I have a last appointment closer to home. Sometimes it is longer. I do many extracurricular activities to get business and, more often, because I am simply so passionate about the many things I do.

Then there is television. While I have not watched any program regularly in more than three decades, I remain a big Philly sports fan.

Living on the east coast means the ending times for games is absolutely ridiculously late. I have decided not to stay up for any games unless they are championship-type games. I need my sleep to stay in shape. I have given up Philadelphia Eagles season tickets as well, in part because I will no longer even watch those Sunday and Monday Night games the Eagles play. There was a Philly kid who made it real big in the NFL or at least played for a number of years. When asked if he grew up an Eagles' fan, he embarrassingly answered that he did not have the time with his sports to keep up with any team. I found that very inspiring. I do not take it anywhere near to that extreme, but my sports and training schedule come first for me, unless it is something like the Phillies in 2008 wining the World Series!

Running and exercise are Blessings in my life, but not without a price. I feel so happy when I overcome the hurdles and keep in shape. It makes the finish line so much sweeter.

What I am perhaps most Grateful for from my almighty doctor experience, is that it has helped me feel the joy of two wonderful things on race or ride day. One is, I know how much work it took for me to get there. Throughout the day I know in the back of my mind is how I have earned the success. It is mine. I feel the Gratitude for getting to the finish line after all I have been through. The second joy is what I feel for other athletes and how much they have gone through to get here. We all share the exhilaration and I admit I am addicted to it.

On a recent triathlon that included many "newbies" (first timers who are always welcomed and celebrated in triathlon world), I saw a man and woman walking together. He was feeling confident that he was actually going to make it. The joy on his partner's face was priceless. How lucky and Blessed I felt to feel that joy of two strangers. It is one of many times I am truly Grateful to feel happiness in others' happiness.

My experience with the almighty doctor also taught me something very vital. While doctors are to be respected, they are not G-d. My attitude towards to the medical community is that you are important to my health, but when I feel you do not value me as a patient it is time to move on. As a volunteer Chaplain, I have seen how much a doctor's bedside manner can make all the difference to a patient when it comes to health.

I have come to cherish Google, etc. for the information they provide. Of great value to us all is to use friends, family and anyone else who can share their knowledge and experience with you for your medical problem. So many friends, family and acquaintances have helped me including a friend who pointed me in the right direction for my orthotics today that saved my running career. Of course, I am one who also treasures all my doctors who have kept me healthy and are a pleasure to be a patient of.

Chapter 13
RESILIENCE LEADS TO EXCELLENCE

My struggle to continue running forced me to look at other sports. Also, a year after we were married, when Gail and I had moved to Dayton, Ohio, I realized it would be very difficult to keep in shape. I decided to buy a bike exerciser for our house. That way whenever I was home, I would have something reliable to use at home. I chose the Schwinn XR-5 bike exerciser based on Consumer Reports rating it highly and suggesting that it could last forever. I made the life enhancing purchase on June 20, 1977, and, with the help of some great bike mechanics, I have been able to keep that amazing machine operating to this very day.

The great thing about cycling is that it does not involve any pounding on the joints. There were no knee or Achilles tendon issues for me to be concerned about. Cycling is wonderful for aerobic workouts and the machine eventually encouraged me to get a regular bike that I could use outside in warmer weather. Cycling is actually where my journey to discover endurance events was born, as I will discuss in "The Big Ride."

While my bike exerciser was fine for home use, it did not help me much when I was on the road. To solve that problem, I began swimming. Whenever I was away, I made sure I would find a hotel or motel with an outside pool in warmer months and an indoor pool during cooler days. That wasn't an easy thing to do back 1977-78 as there was, of course, no internet for me to use nor was the hospitality industry as into fitness the way it is today. But staying in shape meant so much to me that I found a way and on nights I did not take a customer to dinner, swimming became my form of entertainment. I would always find supermarkets where I would buy something healthy to eat after my swim. It was a lot healthier than hanging out in bars or eating unhealthy foods and spending a lot of money doing it.

I soon noticed that when you swim, you enter another dimension: the water. Things slow down and you have a chance to think about problems in slow motion. Now that I swim during lunch, I am able to approach problems in a different way, often with great results. When I am unable to come up with an answer to a problem, at least I am more relaxed and focused and I believe I owe that to swimming.

In retrospect, those two activities, cycling and swimming, started to define an important part of who I am and how I look at the world. For example, today I am a very light drinker. In a given year I probably drink fewer than thirty alcoholic drinks, mostly beer and wine. I may take two or three shots of vodka per annum. Yet people tell me I am always happy. In addition to being married to the woman of my dreams, much of my high comes from doing endurance sports and all that is associated with them. For about a twenty-four-hour period after a race, I am high from endorphins. I am stressed out about a race typically twenty-four to forty-eight hours before an event, except for a marathon or longer distance bike ride or triathlon. And I love that stress because it is nervous energy that shows me how much I care.

Training for events makes race and ride day such a special day that I get a glow that I often call upon for months or even years afterward. Songs remind me of given events and whenever I pass, or am at someplace where part of a race took place, it brings back joyous memories. Since I do a lot of working out in endurance sports, I just find that I do not need booze to loosen up, or be happy.

During those early days, I also began to look at endurance sports as something more than just a workout. It became a chance to take out my frustrations, problems and sadness. After a bad day at work, or when someone was in the hospital or the like, my workout was where I was in charge. It was as though I was saying to whatever had me down: *You are in my house now! You are going to lose badly. I am not just going to beat you, I will humiliate you. After I trash you in my house, I am*

93

coming to yours and it will be my day, my time!

The workout may not actually change anything about a bad situation, but it always makes me feel better and more determined to take care of what is bothering me.

Then there is the people effect. On race or ride day, I find true love in the way all the entrants are so supportive and the way they delight in their own and each other's accomplishments. At my second half-marathon (Philadelphia Half Marathon 2008), I saw a young couple (easy to be younger than me at these races!) embrace and say to each other "thank you so much" and "I am so proud of you." I actually saw the two on a YouTube video in a long loving embrace. I believe they were either married or life partners. I had just broken three hours for the first time, walking 99+% of it, and yet I felt so great for *them* and *their* triumph. Even if athletes do not speak to each other, the joy everyone shares personally, blends into the joy everyone else feels.

At an expo I was working for The American Cancer Society, I spoke to someone who goes from expo to expo promoting a product. He told me the happiness at the events is contagious. He feels it even though he has never entered any event.

Another benefit of being an endurance athlete is that it breeds good eating habits. When you put your body through that much, you need to make sure you have the fuel to get it done. Read any publication dedicated to endurance athletes and you will find recipes, lists of foods to eat and foods to avoid, and tons of advice on how to get your nourishment so you can compete better. Today there are many coaches out there who can help you do better and avoid injuries. More and more, they are emphasizing how to eat to win. I hope I don't sound as if you must eat only boring and healthy foods. I do not know any athlete, me included, who does not enjoy fun food after a race or ride or long workouts. Most of us love burgers, fries, pizza, desserts, etc. There are, in fact, many accomplished athletes who started because they wanted to eat more and not gain weight. A word of caution to all is needed to be said, though. You can definitely eat more, but not a lot more.

One thing I do find upsetting, is that for all the people I know who are doing these events, there are so many more who not only shun exercise, but are paying the price with poor health. As I will describe in "Joy Amidst the Sadness," there is a horrifying number of people whose health and quality of life are highly impacted in a bad way by not exercising enough and/or by engaging in poor eating habits.

While I am sad for them, I have to admit sometimes it gives me great pride in my choices when I see myself in comparison. I recall many times when I was on the road years ago, that I walked by a bar and saw people drinking, smoking (you could do it then at bars) and gobbling down unhealthy foods. There I would be wearing a bathing suit and with a healthy meal in my room awaiting me. At the conclusion of my third marathon, The Atlantic City Marathon in 2011, I walked through a casino on my way to my car. I wore my medal and bib as I was surrounded by overweight people smoking away going to or coming from gambling. They gave me a look as if I was from another planet. While feeling compassion for them, I do admit I was very proud of myself. Shortly after seeing those folks, I was eating a rather tasty hoagie. I had more than earned it.

Staying healthy is also, I believe, a way of giving thanks to G-d. The reasoning is that G-d gave you your body and you show your Gratitude by taking care of it. I am not perfect in this regard but I try, and that is something I cherish deeply.

Going back to walking through the casino for a minute, I think we are all gamblers whether we like to admit it or not. You can be a perfect specimen of being healthy, but you may have conditions beyond your control that prevent you from living a healthy life. I believe we are not held accountable by the Almighty for things beyond our control, we but do have an obligation to try. One of the many things for which I am Grateful to the Sustainer of Life is that I am able to train and complete so many endurance events.

During those early road trips and the year or so we spent in Dayton, my working out and staying healthy also gave me something else. I felt an empowerment. There I was on the road, keeping my form of kosher, which was never easy and often a challenge. To me doing it was keeping G-d in my life when the temptation and rule of the road always seemed to be just fit in and get your work done.

Relaxation seemed to be found only in bars and restaurants offering nothing but unhealthy food. While it is fine to go to these establishments on occasion, making them a nightly stop eventually will wear you down.

When I was traveling, the emphasis on fitness rooms found in just about every hotel today was almost nonexistent. But I found a way to keep in shape. Today, more than 35 years later, I know that meeting those challenges on the road has contributed mightily to my lifetime of health and fitness. It never fails to feel great.

I mentioned that I turned to the bike machine and swimming when my running gave me pain. When we arrived back home from Dayton in June of 1978, I made it a challenge to swim a mile and eventually I did it. Then on two other occasions, I did a two-mile and a 3-mile swim. As I will discuss in "The Greatest Nation," swimming has been a lifetime sport that I have grown to love even more.

I also took up tennis at various times. By playing tennis I discovered that losing is not such a bad thing, as long as you give the game your all and have fun doing it. I played intense single matches against three different guys who, more often than not, would beat me. In spite of usually losing, I loved the competition and camaraderie as we would grab a drink and food afterward to discuss the match with smiles on all our faces.

OK, I admit it was more fun when I won, but even in losing I felt that competing, in many ways, was winning.

Then there was basketball. I played only a little until the 1980s when a friend asked me to join him for a neighborhood game. I loved it immediately. We would battle and scratch and claw trying to win. What was amazing is that the theme of enjoying the competition and camaraderie was elevated to a new level. We would get very physical until someone would complain or get slightly injured. Suddenly the game would calm down as we all knew we had wives, kids and jobs or businesses to tend to the next day. One of my favorite moments came when my team won and a friend I was guarding became upset. He heaved the basketball against the wall saying an expletive. Before the ball hit the wall he turned to me, smiled and said, "Good game."

There was something else I noticed about basketball concerning me. Compared to the others, I was well below average. But to my amazement, I could not help but take note that my teams did not seem to suffer. As I recall, my teams more often than not would either win or tie as opposed to losing. Many of the players had played on organized teams. I played on similar teams only in my imagination. One way I compensated for my lack of experience was by playing smart. Fouling was a great equalizer. When an opponent was about to beat me for a score, I could foul and stop him. The only penalty was they would get the ball. There was no limit for fouls. That was well known and often joked about.

The beginning of the end of my basketball career came while playing beach volleyball on our stairs with my son, Matt, and a friend. When I went to hit the ball, my pinkie became caught in the stairway causing it to become pulled. I knew it right away and shouted "#$&^% I am not going to be able to play basketball!" Everyone laughed except me.

I went to the doctor and was out for a few weeks. I kept coming back taping up the injured finger, which caused another finger to meet the same fate. I decided to wait until my fingers were totally healed. By then, I was rusty and was not a factor in the game until scoring the last two baskets (you had to win by two) in an overtime game. I was overjoyed!

The next week I was pumped and came out on fire. I hit a tough shot to start the game and could feel that this was going to be an All-Star night. But then I felt a pull in my calf area and took myself out of the game. A few days later I pulled into a parking lot as another car pulled in. The driver motioned me to open my door first. I recognized the passenger and waited for him to get out. He had plates in his forearms. He suffered them a few minutes after my injury on the basketball court. With great reluctance, I decided my career was over. I could feel my body telling me my good luck was about to run out.

Though I had to stop, I am forever Grateful for the experience of playing basketball. It empowered me to come back to a sport I had failed in my youth and be able to enjoy being part of it. When I gave it up at around forty-six years old, I was Grateful for not having a major injury or causing a major injury. It had challenged me and was to be a perfect forerunner for the endurance sports that I enjoy today.

As I look back on my athletic life, I find much of my strength as a person comes from the trials and travails I encountered playing sports and how I overcame each of them. The defeats and frustrations I frequently endured in my youth should have disappeared after I did that 3.9-mile run. I should have felt nothing but joy and the thrill of success afterwards. But when I had problems running, I felt bitterness starting to brew in all parts of my very being. Why after so many years of defeat and frustration could I not just be able to run the way it seemed everyone else could? What did I ever do to deserve this punishment?

It is with great pride and Gratitude that I now look back and see myself as developing a wondrous mindset. My mindset is clueless about what despair and the *woe is me* attitude is all about. With the help of the Almighty, I choose instead to go to "plan B" and many other plans in order to find success in sports. In "Always Losing, Always Hopeful," I go into detail about moving on to that special N Word: Next. Remember, you are only as great as what obstacles you overcome.

The one thing I always demand of any exercise is that it be fun. Yes, you can persevere if you really keep your mind to it, but your chances are not great of staying with it unless you are enjoying what you're doing. With the rise in popularity of running, there are so many running clubs out there. These clubs have spawned many people to make great friendships, and they have helped me and others stay motivated to run. Many love to just take long walks and enjoy the outdoors. There are also walking clubs and some that offer both. Many people will enjoy the thrill of competition such as golf, tennis, racket ball, basketball, etc. Others enjoy outside sports like hiking or skiing. The opportunities to find something you enjoy are endless.

Remember, there is one thing for certain about exercise: There will always be reasons to put it off that sound great. When you overcome those reasons and do exercise, though, you will feel even greater. When you fail to keep it up, that is an opportunity for you to take charge and return. When you do that, your odds of success will grow.

Chapter 14
TIME STANDS STILL

I am the Grateful father of two wonderful kids: Matt and Dan. They are both grown now, but I always call my sons *kids*. As I tell them, it is not in any way derogatory, just deeply loving and affectionate. They are both adopted, although we never have and never will consider them anything but our own flesh and blood. It took us a while to receive them, so when they came, we were truly Grateful for them.

The waiting was very frustrating but worth it. Being a parent instantly changes your life forever. The moment they came into our lives, I invented one of my favorite sayings: *Kids were put on earth to drive their parents crazy. That is why they are so much fun and loveable.*

Being parents would pose the greatest challenge to my athletic career, but ultimately lead me to success beyond my wildest dreams.

Matt came first. We got the call at precisely 6:32p.m., on Friday, June 15, 1984, which also happened to be Gail's thirtieth birthday. Although we knew we might be getting "the call," we decided to go to the shore for the weekend anyway. We had been so disappointed in the past we figured, why not just go away? Whatever happens will happen.

I was in the shower when Gail came in so excited she was unable to talk. I told myself I needed to be the calm one and took the phone from her. Very nonchalantly, I arranged for Matt to be delivered to us the following Monday. I hung up the phone feeling, in addition to great joy, proud of myself for being so calm, cool and collected. That is, until I realized I was naked and standing before numerous, uncovered windows.

We both had a great laugh that was tempered by *what do we do now?* The first thing we did was forget about the shore. The second thing was to make many happy phone calls—there was no Facebook or any social media—to announce the good news.

On the way back home we stopped for a celebratory dinner. We discussed everything we needed to do that weekend to prepare for our first child. Our child! Total panic mixed in with the unbridled joy.

We had been married for a little more than nine years. We were very comfortable living in center city Philly, enjoying a relatively carefree, fun life. That weekend we received the baby furniture we had ordered, purchased diapers, bottles, formula, and a ton of baby clothing. I found it rather funny how small the clothes were and how much you could fit into just one drawer. Yes, you can tell I was totally clueless about what to expect.

That Sunday, the day before we would receive Matt, was Father's Day. We went to a brunch at my parents' home where I challenged my metabolism with a little bit of stress eating.

As I walked into my parents' house, a terrifying thought came over me. *This day is for me!* What was I supposed to do? Could I handle such a life change? Would Gail and I lose all romance? What about supporting our kids? I had heard from many parents, including those with means, how expensive it was to raise kids and then you get hit with college. What was all this not sleeping through the night business that exhausted so many I had spoken to? I became extremely nervous and started to panic. I downed about four drinks of whatever adult beverage I had, but did not get drunk. The booze had no effect on me. I devoured every bit of food in sight and was amazed that I did not gain an ounce. I do not recall ever being so hyper-nervous.

The next day we waited for the second call regarding Matt; the call that said he was ready to be delivered to us. I did a little business and by eleven o'clock that morning, was finished. I had nothing to do but wait. To keep my mind from going crazy, I watched a violent movie. I generally do not like violence unless it has an unreal adventure angle to it like *Bourne Identity*, *Indiana Jones*, or *The Mummy*. I watched something with all too realistic street violence, the kind I generally avoided, but on that day it was perfect for me.

The desk eventually called to say he was bringing us a package. Our condo unit was about 200 feet from the elevator. We waited outside our door until we saw someone bringing Matt draped in a blue blanket. For the first time I experienced time standing still.

I remember walking toward Matt, but do not remember anything but the firsts: taking the first step and holding him for the first time. It was love at first sight for both Gail and me. We took him to the doctor who pronounced him healthy and then parenthood had begun.

There are many people who love the infant stage. For us it was difficult, especially for me. The physical demands were very onerous and wherever you went, it was as if you were moving out an army brigade with all you needed. Going out to dinner became a challenge so we more often than not just ate in. But as Matt learned to recognize us and become an individual with his own, unique personality, we reveled in it all. We loved every stage and of course loved Matt. And I developed a sudden, profound respect for what my parents went through raising me from a totally helpless infant into adulthood.

Children also change your social order. Getting together with others, especially from infanthood through their young childhood, becomes a whole different set of norms. Babysitters become your lifeline to the outside world. You have them: you can go out. You do not: you stay in.

With any adoption there is always a worry that the birth parents may change their minds. In our case, Gratefully, this did not happen with either Matt or Dan. When Matt was about six months old, we went to Family Court in Philadelphia to finalize the adoption. The event took place in a small room before a wonderful Judge who had an adult kid living across the street from us. As the fast proceedings ended, he asked my mother in a very serious way: "Are you going to do your job?" She became very nervous until he smiled and said, "Spoil the grandchild." With such ease and happiness, he was officially ours forever.

When Matt was three, we moved from an awesome center city high rise, the Dorchester, to a home just outside the city, where we still live. The decision was made when Matt, around age one, ran into a neighbor's door. She opened it and laughed. But we asked ourselves what would happen when he was ten and runs into a door with a couple of his buddies?

Our center city days were replaced with the quiet life of suburban Lower Merion Township. Our house there is actually located just around the corner from where I grew up. I love the area and we are very happy here.

When Matt went to preschool we developed a whole new set of friends based upon his new friends. We fit right in and, again, loved that stage of our lives. Seeing Matt grow was something to be Grateful for and cherish every day, no matter what issue would come up. Of course there was a saying we completely bought into: *little kids, little problems, big kids, big problems.*

At that time the family business was humming along and we lived a very comfortable and secure life financially. I was involved in running the business' real estate and very much enjoyed it. Our house was perfect for us and so was our neighborhood. Life settled into a wonderful routine with Gail and me alternating in taking care of Matt. I kept in shape by cycling, swimming, walking, and playing some tennis. But as in anyone's life journey, things always change and sometimes that means they become more challenging. That would be the case with us.

In November 1988, I received a message to call the person who had arranged for us adopting Matt. I learned we had three days before another son, Dan, would arrive. In parenthood another child does not just increase your workload arithmetically, but geometrically as well. At least that's what we learned.

With the second child, parents often feel things are suddenly routine, that they know what to expect when they give birth or, in our case, adopt. How wrong that was for us!

No one brought Dan to us. We went to the hospital to pick him up. On the way, we told ourselves we would be very professional about the whole process. We'd go in with that mindset, keep things moving along, do what we had to do, and then get Dan to the same doctor who had seen Matt right away. Happily such a routine and serious event would not be the case. When we saw Dan for the first time, we again fell in love instantly. We couldn't do anything but stand there and admire him the way we did with Matt. We did eventually move it along—at the prodding of the nurse. The doctor soon told us Dan was healthy and normal.

Dan's adoption process was much different from Matt's as well. It was held in a full-blown court room and was very formal. There was no joking judge presiding but that didn't matter. Gail and I still felt the unbridled joy that came with knowing he was officially our child.

As any parent knows, two small children is a challenge. You want to make the baby welcomed but not at the expense of the attention you give to your older child. We worked hard at the balance. We showered love to both of our amazing kids to make sure there would be no jealousy. For us, that also included accepting each of them for who they are and acknowledging their totally different personalities. They do share a few commonalities: they both love sports (Philly teams of course!), they love each other, and they love us.

Matt is very intellectual, but often cannot figure out how to do the mundane. While he has numerous friends, you will not see him being the life of the party. He has a very strong moral character, he reads a lot, and he knows what is going on in the world. Presently, he takes care of my granddaughter Annabel and another little girl, and does tutoring for SATs. He is married to Hannah, who is doing well as a Methodist Minister. We heard her speak at a graduation recently and were totally amazed. They both have a strong sense of doing what is right. And we have a great love for Hannah and her family. I once heard that you instantly love your grandchild and then get to know her/him with unbridled pride and joy. Annabel has a wonderful personality, is always happy and loves people and dogs. How Blessed Gail and I feel.

Dan has always been everyone's friend. We would go to a public place and more kids would say *hello* to him than the rest of us. Dan has a great sense of direction and can figure out the ins and outs of a place within minutes of arriving. When he was very young, still in the single digits, he discovered he loved to create art and design projects, like once he created an artist's rendering for a golf hole. And he loves the game of golf, in part because of its social nature. Dan started out at an academic college. One day he realized he wanted to try the art world in the areas of graphic and industrial design. Dan is now excelling in a program for the arts, and doing great on an internship. My 65th birthday was spent moving him back from Austin, Texas to home. It is a joy to have him back home. A quick shout out for Austin, Texas. Great town but love having Dan back.

We are so proud of our gentlemen sons (I use the term rather loosely, but affectionately) and for how well they are doing in their lives. They were always nice kids and were always polite and respectful to everyone. As Gail and I often said, we treated them with respect and they gave it back to us. On the very few occasions they were disrespectful, all we had to do was give them a disapproving look and they would change their tune. In return, we'd give them a very approving look.

It's probably no surprise that some of the fondest memories I have of Matt and Dan involve going to sports games with them. I have had numerous ticket arrangements with each of them and while none of our teams ever won a championship, I was with Matt when the Flyers clinched making it to the Stanly Cup Finals in 1997, and I saw the Eagles win the NFC championship for the 2004 season with Dan.

Our luck was not better for the teams they played on, except for one magical season. We considered their personal sports our family team. As such, our family record for soccer was four wins, thirty-three losses and one tie. We had a streak of fifteen straight losses that was eventually broken by Dan's team. Matt was at that game. It was a very rare, convincing win for our team. We were so excited we all went to another section of the field so we could rejoice, yell, and scream together.

Despite the many losses, I always jumped at the opportunity to coach their sports teams whenever it was presented. While we lost many games, the bonding was something I deeply cherish and am Grateful for.

The losses changed in 2001 during that magical season I briefly mentioned earlier. Dan had joined a roller hockey team that had one amazing player and a smart coach. The coach quickly discovered Dan was great at defense. He was the first team defense on June 6, 2001, when they won the league championship. It was awesome. The joy and confidence it brought were life enhancing for Dan, not to mention for his long-suffering father. The memory of Dan skating around with unrestrained happiness is one of my greatest life memories. It was such a Gift from the Almighty. I was and am deeply Grateful.

Thirteen days after Dan won his roller hockey championship, Matt and I went on our first training bike ride that wound up initiating my journey on the road to numerous championship moments and ultimately led to one of the two reasons for my name *Attitude of Gratitude*. In June of the previous year, I was a recreational, very casual cyclist doing typically twelve or so miles from our Beach House in Atlantic City to Longport and back. I once did two loops for a total of about twenty-two miles and promptly got a cramp in my quads.

At a family get-together with Gail's sister, a friend of hers spoke about the American Cancer Society Bike-a-Thon, a sixty-one mile ride. My son, Matt, and I were intrigued. We could not do the ride that year since there was a wonderful wedding on my side of the family that weekend. But we both decided to ride the following year.

As the weather warmed up in 2001, I called the family friend for some advice. He told me to join a team with a captain. We registered and did a little fundraising. My letter about *61 miles on a bike* did more than just raise some money to fight cancer. It gave me a new passion. And, for the first time in my life, I was an athlete that people were paying attention to and talking about. While it was a light-year away from the athletes we follow in major or even minor sports, it brought me such pride and contentment. For me, the event was the "big time" in sports that had been denied me in my youth. While I did not call it Gratitude at the time, I was profoundly Grateful to the Almighty for this Gift of being able to do such a challenge with my beloved son.

I strongly suspected that many people wanted to do the ride but they did not train much for it, or train much at all. We were not that way. On June 19, 2001, not quite two weeks after Dan's championship roller hockey game, Matt and I decided to ride the Schuylkill River Trail for around thirty miles. We rented Matt a bike to see it was something he wanted to do before we actually purchased one. And for me it was a test as to whether I could handle longer distances. That life changing day we did 29½ miles(!) and both collapsed when we got home. That would be the only long distance ride we ever would feel such exhaustion. We were ready and raring to do whatever training necessary for what became known as the *Big Ride*. I will go into much more detail about what that meant to me in "The Big Ride" chapter.

In many ways June of 2001 was a turning point in our lives. Dan was increasingly independent and Matt was close to going to college. Being their parent with the love of my life Gail, was what life was all about. Watching two lumps (that is what we affectionately called our kids as infants) become great adult human beings is something for which I will be forever Grateful.

Being a parent is something you seemingly have so much control over as your children grow up. But you never know how they will turn out until they become adults. There have been so many instances of parents whom everyone deemed "bad," whose kids turned out to be great and vice versa. The reason is simple: your baby will grow into an adult with his or her own mind but luck is often involved in how things will actually turn out for them.

We are all gamblers at the table of life. Parents never know what will interest their children and how those interests will affect their lives. Who will they meet that could have an influence on them? Will that impact create a positive or negative direction in their life? As a parent all you can do is do your best and pray for the best for them.

Chapter 15
SURVIVING AND THRIVING
WHEN THE WORST THING HAPPENS

To back up a little, in the early nineties, around the time Matt was about eight and Dan was four, ominous clouds in our life started to appear regarding our financial life. The family business had always been a great source of both money and status. While Gail and I had never been social climbers or one of those couples consumed with their egos, feeling entitled to being waited on, we did enjoy the status of being part of one of the Philadelphia's most successful family businesses. The financial strength of the business meant tremendous freedom from the typical worries about housing, kids' education, retirement, etc. We did not have to concern ourselves with those stresses in life much at all.

But looking back, there were danger signs all over the place in our business. On the manufacturing end, we had reached a point of being too small to be big, and too big to be small. On the real estate end, we were making great money selling assets, but were unable to replace them. And then the market tanked. We were stuck with properties that were not sellable and that were costing us money. In one of the most ridiculous moves by a city, Philadelphia suddenly required fire sprinklers for office buildings but not apartment buildings. While in retrospect if it made sense for office buildings, why would it not have made even more sense for apartment buildings? People sleep in apartments; they do not in office buildings generally (at least they are not supposed to).

Our business had been around for more than seventy-five years and was slowly in the process of closing down. We did have the strength not to ask *why us?* As the years had gone by, we had watched the business world change with lightning speed. Today businesses rise to great heights and in a matter of years are out or closed down because the world moves so fast. Examples abound such as fax machines, movie rental stores, bookstores, VCR's, etc. It was pretty amazing that we had lasted for seventy-five years.

As we faced our future wondering how to afford the basics of living in an affluent area, we had much on our plate to be concerned about. Gail had left teaching after eight years to become a residential real-estate agent, starting with the purchase of our magnificent home. She stayed on but did not become all that involved as she was forced to deal with the break-up of our family business. While she had been one of the most successful agents in a very competitive area, it had taken a toll on her. Residential, rarely if ever, takes a day off. Nights and weekends are the norm. When you are dealing with what, for most people, is their biggest asset—where they happen to live— emotions run high. Gail had not only enjoyed success but has an impeccable reputation and integrity. What I will be forever Grateful for is not once did she, in anyway put me down for the situation we were faced with, something that was never supposed to happen.

The worst loss for us was our beach house in Atlantic City. The memories of that place were among the most happy and cherished. Today we again have a phenomenal condo with a breathtaking view, but we know how much we missed in Matt and Dan's formative years by not having our beach house. Life is about moving on, and we have done that with our love for the Jersey Shore and we now love every minute we spend there. In fact, a great percentage of this book was written overlooking the Atlantic Ocean.

While Gail had a place to go to earn money, I was for the first time in my life entering the nonfamily-business job market. After almost twenty years of working in the family business, while I did not own it, I had the pleasure of receiving plenty of perks along with a rather nice salary every year from it. The most logical path for me to take was to go into real estate, but at that time the area was experiencing a deep recession in real estate. My first focus was to try being a real estate broker. At that time there was a rather cushy office and some office buildings that my family wanted to lease or sell. The market for selling them was nonexistent, so I thought I'd try finding tenants.

Leasing proved to be as difficult as selling. We had class C buildings that we had renovated to be good alternatives for smaller users, who wanted their own floor, a decent location and lower rents. We started out doing pretty well with those rents, but when the market crashed for office space, our tenants discovered they could pay the same price at class A buildings. Hence we had vacancies. The deals of the day required us to spend about three years' worth of rent up front, for a five-year lease give or take. The financial strength of the potential tenants suggested that in a year they would be no more, thus leaving us with spending two years' worth of rent we would not collect. To further cause us angst was that city requirement to spend a small fortune putting in sprinklers as soon as we got new tenants. Their logic was understandable: in theory we would be in the money so it was a good time to improve our building. Crying hardship was not an option.

The very companies I wanted to go to as a broker, made it clear that the only reason they would want me was that I could bring the listings of our buildings. My concern was what would happen after those spaces were sold or leased up? Would I still have a job? Probably not. Besides, those firms were not the ones I really wanted to go to for a variety of reasons. As a broker, today I fully understand why the brokerage community was very cool to me coming aboard. In their eyes, I was the fat cat who had spent his career resting in his cushy office never spending any money so I probably had no idea what the market was really about.

When I did manage to get an interview, there was often a personality test I had to take to see if commercial real estate brokerage would fit my personality. Twice I failed to make the grade. I found it funny because the test was right when figuring out my character traits and yet that supposedly meant I was not fit to be a broker.

In addition to being a real estate broker, I tried to become an executive at a local company. When that went nowhere, I tried getting a sales position. In May of 1994 I was "successful" at landing a job selling chemicals. The company's strategy for selling those wonderful products (yes, there is sarcasm there) was to put on a great demonstration and then offer awards for buying. The first day out training with my manager, I was told to stay away from the business owners because they did not want to spend money. That was the first of many red flags about that job. In fact, there were so many that I could write another book on it. But by that time I was desperate to start working again, so I took the job with great trepidation. I was told from the beginning that many salespeople made over $100,000.

The job itself was demeaning. You had to carry a big bag with all your demonstration equipment in it along with a price book. Receptionists saw me a mile away and well over half the time I was thrown out before getting anywhere (and that was even when I had a gift for the receptionist).

About two months into my sales career with that company, I was sent to headquarters for a three-day intensive training program. At lunch I sat next to the President of the company and tried to relate to him from my days at my family business.

It was obvious he was uneasy being in the room with us. And as soon as he had the opportunity to leave, he did so, casting a look of disgust at me. It was as if he was saying *shut up and sell.*

At dinner they wanted to know if we had any questions. I asked how many sales people actually made over $100,000. Uncomfortably, they said, "quite a lot." Then one finally said, "We think it is over one third." My manager later let it slip that really only five out of three hundred made that much money. I deduced the success stories at this company came from those who lived in rural areas, where businesses and institutions are not bombarded with as many visitors as they'd receive in metropolitan areas and they were more likely to buy something just to be nice.

I still took great pride in that conference. Most of my fellow sales people were enthusiastic about this company, but I was not. They may have had me due to my difficult situation, but they could not fool me. After seven months, I left. It would have been sooner but they charged you for the sales products you were to use. It took a couple of months for me to get rid of it all while I continued looking for a better opportunity. Several years later I read about how one of those $100,000 sales persons turned state's evidence in a lawsuit about fraudulent selling. Good riddance.

The era of job insecurity was the most challenging time in my adult life. All the charitable and political groups I was involved with ended at that time, including the AIPAC, Golden Slipper, Anti-Defamation League, Jewish Community Relations Council, and Federation Allied Jewish Appeal. The last thing I wanted was to have to cut back due to job loss, but when I saw the handwriting on the wall with our business, I "retired for the duration of childrearing." It was the only way I knew how to save face. It hurt deeply to have to do it but having two wonderful kids and the love of my life as a wife softened that blow.

Outside the home, though, in business situations or when I'd see people in public places like kids' games, shopping, or social situations was another matter. Everyone, to me, seemed as if they were doing better than I was and had a greater future than I did. I was extremely uncomfortable discussing anything related to business. What could I say? Telling people you were closing up was not high on my list of subjects to make public for a lot of reasons.

The first thing you do at a time like that in your life is to do what is commonly called networking. I met with numerous people from just about every angle in my life. Most were very supportive and tried to be helpful. I am deeply Grateful to them for the kindness they gave me at that vulnerable point in my life.

There were a (very) few contacts, though, where the only Gratitude I have is that I did not let their reaction to me tear me down. Someone was surprised I had called him. He said sarcastically, "If you have the guts to call me, you will find something," and hung up. There were three who looked at me as if I had leprosy and they did not want to catch it from me: economic failure. In a sense I am Grateful for them being the way they were because their behavior showed me how mentally tough I am and what I had to overcome. G-d Blessed me with a lot of inner strength and fortitude that I did not know I ever had. And Gail's support was my foundation for never giving up on the situation or me.

Also helping me along the way were the very many people who showed me compassion when I really needed it. I learned how much a kind word or gesture can help someone. I received countless words of encouragement and every one of them means so much to me still. Whenever someone would compliment me during that tough time, it would make my day. Smiles and recalling good times spent together with many I met, would also bolster me.

Then came the night at synagogue when there was an activity involving our kids. Since I was coming back late that evening, I had planned to meet my family at temple. They were late also so I waited in the sanctuary alone. Eventually, a group of highly successful families gathered around me. I should have gotten up and walked to the lobby but I had had a tough day of networking failure along with more bad news about the family business. For the first time ever, I felt I did not deserve anything better in life. For what seemed like hours, I sat feeling more and more inadequate.

Then a friend spotted me and said magic words: "Roy, come sit with us. We have seats for you all." I jumped at the chance to get out of the dark place I was in. The rest of the night was wonderful. I am forever in debt to that friend whose very simple act of kindness brought me out of a hole.

That kind act had further ramifications. The next day, I started to think about the wonderful reception everyone gave me when I had gone over to sit with them. I decided I would never again allow myself to be put in such a situation like that. Just because I was not the most successful business person, did not mean I deserved to be surrounded by those who made me uncomfortable. People care about me and I care about them. That makes me worth something. Then I realized how important it is to be compassionate with myself. Always remember, when you are struggling, you need to be upbeat with yourself. The world may be kicking you down, but at least *you* can be cheering for yourself.

Too many times in our society we see people losing all sense of self-worth because they lose a job or business. What do we usually answer when asked: "what do you do?" We usually reply with what it is we do for a living, as if our jobs are what make us who we are as humans. If you have a job, business, or career, please remember that

113

and realize how much a kind word or two could mean to someone out there looking for a job.

That empowering incident sparked a very positive evaluation for how I would view negativity in my life, when there was anything to be negative about. The time had come for me to put an end to the toxic people I would come into contact with. If someone was not only unhelpful to me but also insulting, it was time for me to put them out of my life. Think about it: if someone kicks another when they are down, that person must have issues they are dealing with. So instead of feeling anger, resentment, and looking for revenge, why not just write them off?

The saying I heard about *bearing a grudge is like letting someone you do not care for live in your head rent free* became my personal rallying cry. I also started to think about another saying: *living well is the best revenge.*

As I replayed in my head all the contacts who were meanest to me, I realized they seemed to have worries of their own about their wealth and position. They did not want to be reminded by my presence that what had happened to me could ever happen to them. It was as though I could be contagious.

In those bad times, I really started to appreciate even more my family, friends and associates who were upbeat to be around. In the back of my mind I started to see my future of when I would be doing well again. I promised myself I would remember how positivity can help so many. Today I love to, and am very Grateful that I am able to lift up people's spirits whenever the opportunity presents itself. Doing so is also a perfect reminder of how I was able to overcome such a difficult period in my life.

Rather than wanting payback against anyone, I think about how I overcame their negative vibes and am far stronger for it. I wonder if any of them could have done what I did. The best thing, though, is I do not care! But, if it did happen to them, I would wish them well and might even help them. Yes, I admit I would not go overboard, but I know I would not delight in their tough times.

Prayer was another way I coped when things were rough. During the Jewish High Holidays, the Assistant Rabbi, when we were members of Har Zion, gave a sermon that inspired me to go to Friday morning services every week. Those services are typically called minyan. Minyan, again, means there must be ten Jews (men for the Orthodox) for the gathering to be considered complete. The main reason for meeting on Friday mornings is to say *Kaddish*, a prayer for the dead. I have seen in so many cases that saying *Kaddish* every day for a loved one is an amazing way to cope with grief. The support you get in any synagogue is always warm and comforting but it is there with the *Kaddish* when mourners start, in many ways, to live again. You never get over the death of a loved one but you do heal and are able to live again while never forgetting your loved one.

One of the things about Judaism I love now but I didn't use to, is something called an unveiling. That is when you unveil a gravestone to formally end the mourning period, which typically lasts eleven months. I used to think it was cruel to bring up such sad memories, but I now find it a great way to heal. On the anniversary of your loved one's death, you say *Kaddish* and then you say it during three other holidays during the year, at *Yizkor*, a memorial service for the dead.

When I started to go to minyan on Friday mornings, I was in the process of a different type of mourning; it was the death of the family business. My life was changing and I was very unsure of how things would work out. At minyan I found unspoken support. I have always found at services that there are people who go for their own situation. Whether saying it or not, they come to pray to G-d for help and support. The atmosphere has an unspoken sheltering, supportive embrace for everyone. I know this is true about every synagogue I have ever entered, as well as all the Churches I have been in. That silent support was just what I needed at the time. No one was judging me and I could feel the warmth that emanated to everyone.

Going to minyan also helped me to pray and unleash my innermost thoughts and fears to the Almighty One Blessed Be He. In asking for His Blessing to find me a business opportunity, I started to ask for it for reasons other than just for me. I asked G-d to help so I could be a better father and husband, to be a better person to everyone I would come into contact with, and to serve the Almighty. I found great comfort in my prayers not being purely selfish but with a purpose.

Shortly after going to minyan, I learned about tefillin, the leather straps and boxes you bind around your arm and head. The tradition comes from Deuteronomy 6:5 where Jews are told: "And Thou shalt bind them as a sign upon thine hand and they shall be as frontlets between thine eyes." In other words, tefillin is a symbol of one's intentions to be bound to prayer. I restarted my habit of praying just about every day then. The combination of synagogue and personal prayer to this day is a practice I am deeply Grateful to G-d for.

Today, I use prayer in the morning for numerous reasons. Prayer is a way to step back and think about what is really important to you. It is a time to give thanks for things we take for granted. When we acknowledge them, it is a way to feel special and loved. You will also feel obligated to do something good for all you have been given. Doing an act of kindness more often than not brings very positive things into your life.

At times when I am upset, I pour out my innermost thoughts and plead to G-d in prayer. In return, I have always felt some comfort, even if G-d did not grant me what I was asking for. In such cases, I feel G-d is at least giving me the strength to get through a tough time.

I had three experiences in synagogue that I want to share with you that can only be described as what some call, *G-d Moments*. On February 27, 2004, Gail had a mammogram that showed breast cancer in the back of her breast. Today, she has survived and thrived for more than twelve years being cancer free. She only needed radiation. On the first Friday minyan I went to after learning about her illness, as I walked into the chapel I felt a warmth come over my heart, mind, body and soul. I believe G-d was telling me that no matter what, I could always come here or pray to Him wherever and whenever.

The second time it happened was the first Rosh Hashanah after the passing of my beloved father. The night before we had a very celebratory holiday dinner that was festive and happy for everyone except me. I wondered why until I walked into synagogue the next day. That's when I realized I missed my father for the first time—not the man who was sick in his later life, but the vibrant and jovial man he was before he became ill with heart disease that would ultimately take him from us. I felt the warmth was G-d's way of saying my father's soul was bound up in the bonds of eternal life.

The third time was when our dynamic and inspiring Rabbi at temple Adath Israel piped in a closed telecast for home- and hospital-bound folks during the high holidays in 2013. As Rabbi explained what we were doing and wished the viewers well, I became very sad for all my patients in the hospital at that time of year. But then I felt so Grateful that I could feel their pain. In "Joy Amidst the Sadness" I will go into detail about how my work as a volunteer Chaplain is fulfilling the mitzvah (Divine Commandment) of *bikur cholim* (visiting the sick) and how it is something I feel G-d has blessed me with. Me not performing anything other than the joy and privilege of serving Him.

Temple Adath Israel, under the leadership of our Rabbi, Assistant Rabbi and Canter, has created a loving, supportive community. Rabbi is one of the most inspiring speakers I have ever heard. He also has an amazing ability with kids. Anyone who calls a Shabbat (Sabbath) for kids "Shabbat Shabang," just gets it. And he can dazzle a service. Many, including Jews, do not know that Yom Kippur, the Day of Atonement when we fast, is actually a day of solemn joy: we are about to be Forgiven. Rabbi is able to remind us of that to the point where he once had me dancing in the aisles with my mother during a Yom Kippur service.

I felt that sense of community the first time I walked into a Friday morning minyan service. Not only that, but I also discovered I belonged there for another reason. The lay leader happened to sit in front of me that morning. Everyone came over and hugged him. I could not help but say, "You have one warm and welcoming synagogue." He laughed and told me he had just arrived back from Israel where he took a week-long bike ride. As my eyes lit up, he recognized me as the co-chair of Bike-a-Thon. Naturally, we became fast friends.

However, not only did I have a fellow, kindred, bike-riding spirit at temple, I had a whole supportive network. One of the great things about the minyan is that a breakfast follows. It is sponsored by a congregant or two and is a perfect time to mingle and speak with each other. I often mention some endurance event I am doing. The support the others give me touches me with great joy and happiness.

Minyan brought my prayers to a whole new level and perhaps paved the way for what I'm about to discuss in the next chapter, "The Fax That Changed My Life." My praying was about to set me on a new course that is the basis for my Attitude of Gratitude.

Chapter 16
THE FAX THAT CHANGED MY LIFE

Today, now that I am long past my struggles related to the end of our family business, I can view that era as a source of strength and character building. However, there was a point where I thought I would never get over it. That time of my life is arguably the most challenging and difficult one of my adult life. At my lowest point, I pictured myself losing everything and not just the business. I thought Gail would take the kids and be embarrassed to even call me her ex.

As I look back I am truly amazed how low we can sink in our own mind when the situation, while dire, is not the end of the world. Again I hear my father's wonderful words: *For better or worse this too shall pass.*

I mentioned earlier that our problem in the business boiled down to two things. First we were too big to be small and too small to be big. What I mean by that is that many privately held companies do very well with the owner(s) wearing all the hats to get things done. They are able to run around their bigger competition by offering better service. That is how we started.

But as we grew, we developed huge overhead costs that forced us into an arena of battling it out with larger companies. We chose to take a pass on the investment required to make changes for numerous reasons. Instead, we started selling our manufacturing businesses and we liquidated one of them. I was rather pleasantly surprised by how much money we made on selling machinery for a business that had long ago run its course.

The second problem with the business was our model for real

estate that had worked so well that we fell victim to changing times. Renovating older office buildings was a great idea for us for many years. But the recession of the early 90s doomed our buildings. As I've already described, our tenants could go to higher class buildings for about the same price they paid us, so our buildings emptied. In short, they were obsolete and in need of retrofitting that would cost a lot of money. It's interesting to note that today most of our buildings are now residential, mimicking the trend from office to residential that is happening in many parts of the country.

As we lost tenants, I felt helpless in many ways. I questioned myself as to why I could not come up with something to save the day. Now that I have witnessed many businesses rise and fall in a just few short years, I know when looking back that it was all inevitable. There was nothing about it that should make me feel like a failure. Our family business was a legacy that was about to expire. I was just one of the leaders who could not save it.

Gail, Matt, and Dan had grown used to seeing me as a successful businessman. Our friends and a multitude of good acquaintances also saw me as a model, a "pillar of the community." Gail had come from a modest socio-economic background into the world of my family business. I worried how people would view me once the business would cease to exist. What charity or other cause I was involved with would want anything to do with me? And suddenly going into work was, for the first time in my life, something I dreaded. What would it be like working for someone else?

With all of that was going on, I started to look at where I was as a person. The most painful realization I came to was that I felt entitled in many ways to being wealthy forever, and that nothing could ever get in my way. I also have to admit I had gotten away from my Judaism at that point and was starting to feel like nothing bad could ever happen to me.

Although I have never considered myself a snob, I do admit in the years leading up to the end of the family business, I felt myself to be superior. That loss of humility was something I had to admit to and work to improve.

Praying every day and trying to serve the Almighty fulfills something Judaism calls *Tshuvah*, which means repentance or return.

For me, the return was to come back to being a spiritual person and trying to serve the Creator of all life by serving those created in His Image. As painful as that time was, I am Grateful for how it made me a better, happier person in spite of the fact that I did not have the money or status I had during the days we had a family business.

One of the many things I love about Passover, the story of the Israelites being redeemed from slavery to be G-d's chosen people, is the purifying effect the experience had on the Jewish people. By going through so much suffering and wandering, we became ready to accept the Torah (the Five Books of Moses) and strive to become a Light Unto the Nations from the Holy Land, the modern State of Israel. The purification I was going through was nothing in any way to compare to what the Israelites (my ancestors) went through, nor what all too many others in human history had gone through. But it was a major turning point in my life. Humility is a good thing when it spurs one on to admit mistakes and to resolve to improve oneself. But humility when it causes a person to sink to the point where they view themselves as worthless and incorrigible is not good in anyway.

As December 1992 approached, I was at that low, incorrigible, point. My networking to find a new job or business was going nowhere and in a few cases presented great challenges to keep my self-confidence from falling into an abyss. We were at the point where Gail had to work crazy hours and with people buying or selling the greatest asset they had. The stress was constant. As I looked at going into real estate brokerage, I found nothing but obstacles. Gail never let me feel low about us being in that situation, and for that I am forever Grateful to her. In the tough times you find out what your spouse is made of. I was truly blessed to have Gail as my wife and I still am to this day.

While in the depths of the desperation related to the family business situation, within my psyche anything that went wrong, was exacerbated and I had trouble concentrating. On some relatively minor matters, I made mistakes that were totally uncharacteristic of me. One of those mistakes seemed apparent when, as part of a deal to sell out our interest in a development to our partner, we were given four upscale lots to sell and Gail was chosen as the agent.

We had planned to visit New York City right before New Year's where we would stay in my parents' apartment. As we were getting ready to leave for the trip up, Gail found a buyer for the lots. What great news! But my elation was broken when Gail asked me a question her buyer had: "What about steep slope?" A steep slope means you can only disturb a certain defined amount of sloped ground, or land that is hilly, which was just about the entire parcel.

My heart sank. I knew there was something about that issue five years earlier but I was totally clueless at the time of the potential sale and caught off guard.

I did know we had only a certain amount and if we had no more left, the lots were worthless. If that was the case, I would have been the cause of us being swindled by my incompetence. Worse yet, I would embarrass Gail. I worried so much, one night I dreamed she left me, taking Matt and Dan with her to get away from me, the biggest loser in the world.

Our trip was planned for December 28 or 29. The offer came in just after the Christmas holiday. In a panic, I called our engineer, expecting him to laugh in my face calling me a total moron and idiot. He was not there. He was gone until after New Year's. I would be unable to enjoy our trip, but I was resolved not to ruin it for my family. I told myself to keep my worry under wraps and that whatever the pain would be like, in no way would I let on to anyone else. As we drove up to New York, I was satisfied I would not get in anyone's way of a good time.

We parked the car and walked up to my parents' apartment. Gail went in first to turn the lights on. Matt and Dan ran in to watch TV. And I brought in the luggage wondering whether I could figure out how to connect video game system for them (very difficult for me!).

But then my life changed forever and the foundation of this book was laid.

Gail casually told me there was a fax on the floor and that it looked like it was for me. I picked it up. The fax was a copy of a letter sent to me and our partner about five years prior that detailed the precise amounts of steep slope used and that were left. We had more than enough. The lots would sell easily.

Because of that fax, all the stress about steep slope Gratefully left me. I went into the other room and broke down and cried to G-d, "*Baruch Hashem.*" Blessed is the Almighty. I cried for several minutes thanking G-d again and again. I dried my eyes and told Gail, "This is about steep slope. Do you want it?" Gail told me to put it away, forget about any business for now and just enjoy our family.

That was one amazing trip! I loved every minute of it including having to figure out how to hook up the video games, being in crowded and noisy places, and dealing with the cold. It did not matter that I had been liberated from the burden of worrying about steep slope. I thought G-d's gift to me was somehow having our engineer calling his office and having his secretary send a copy of the steep slope letter to quickly deal with a minor manner.

Before the end of January 1993, I would discover the Gift the Almighty gave me was actually something far more precious and life changing. One day I walked by one of our files and decided I should check out the old file on the development that involved steep slope. To my surprise I found a file with "steep slope" written in my handwriting (very easy to recognize as it is the one most illegible). The file had only one piece of paper: the same letter the engineer had sent me with a note I made saying, "Plenty of steep slope. Not anything to be worried about." I had worried about something I had taken care of five years earlier and forgotten about because it was nothing to be concerned about.

Instead of being upset with myself for needless worry, I used this as a pick me up. I started to gain more confidence in myself and stopped taking all the blame for our family business' imminent closing. More importantly, I started to discover my Attitude of Gratitude. While I did not call it that at the time, my praying increased and became more focused on all I had to be Grateful for.

When I would meet with someone looking for a new opportunity, I would be Thankful that I handled myself well and that they treated me nicely. Little things started to bring me great pleasure as I would acknowledge my Gratitude for them. Suddenly, I was Grateful for our home and family, friends whom I enjoyed being around, anyone I would come into contact with whom I enjoyed if only for a brief moment, and the good health of my loved ones.

At that time I was also praying every day. On Saturday, the Jewish Sabbath, I gave thanks for Blessings received during the week. These included good weather, any upbeat meetings, being with family and friends, my good health and the ability to work out, the material things we had and with great Gratitude I always add, *etc.!*

Despite all of my struggles there was so much to be Grateful for. The joy of those prayers led me to discover how wonderful you feel when you look at what you have instead of at what you do not have.

One of the best moments showing me how well my new attitude was working for me happened during a particularly difficult weekend. I was facing a very tough business decision in the coming week. It is not important what it was, only to know how stressed I was. At that time when we would go out, I would typically have two drinks and no more unless it was a special occasion. That weekend the only peace I knew was drinking two Bloody Mary's. They tasted so good and I loved being relaxed. When the second drink was wearing off the waiter asked if I wanted a refill. I knew if I would drink it, I would feel better that day, but have to face the next day with a hangover. I refused and knew I would never have a drinking problem.

Another benefit of my Gratitude is that I started to find more things to take off the stress. At the time I was playing basketball with some friends once a week. As my situation became more difficult in dealing with my business future, I appreciated those games as a way to release the stress I had. People who made me feel better, I tried to see more of and vice versa with people who did not make me feel so good. I am very Grateful those latter types are far and few between in my life.

I started to do other things, too, that would make me feel better. For example, I would intentionally concentrate more on the fun things I did with my kids, like watching Philly sports, in lieu of worrying.

My prayers also started to ask G-d that I find something worthwhile to do His Will and be a great example of a good person doing well, as a way to help others improve themselves. To be able to follow through on my end, I resolved to become a more compassionate person, which is an ongoing project for me.

During that time, I revisited my kosher observance and rededicated myself to keeping kosher style. I chose to refrain from eating pork and shellfish and not to mix meat, including poultry, with dairy. Once again, the rules work for me by always reminding me of the Will of G-d being the most important thing we need to consider. I realize I am far from perfect, but I try.

The purification I went through at the time as, with my ancestors in ancient Egypt—albeit on a much smaller and easier scale—involved me losing my arrogance and sense of entitlement. Even though I had very little of it, I did have it.

But then I wondered whether I could ever succeed on my own. The answer is a resounding *yes*! As I will describe in "Always Losing, Always Hopeful," I have found success in being a commercial real estate broker for business and a personal life filled with purpose, success and happiness. And it all started with me discovering Gratitude.

When you concentrate on how much you have, you tend to feel very Blessed and therefore happy. A happy disposition helps one in the workplace. I am in sales and I know that the better mood I have going into any meeting, the more likely it will be successful for me. And the happier you are, the more you attract others to be in your corner as a friend or someone who will just give you positive vibes. I have often gone into a retail establishment of some kind and walked out happier because of a wonderful interaction with someone helping me, taking my money or even a fellow customer.

That fax in December 1992 showed me the joy of Gratitude. It changed the way I view the world. Whenever I am down, which is rare, I start to think of all I have to be Grateful for and feel the warmth of one of the Almighty's greatest gifts to us all: Gratitude.

Too often people in challenging times forget about all the good in their life and only think about the bad. It is not easy to redirect that focus, I know. And there are times when you may find yourself in really bad circumstances. But trust me, it is always possible to find

Gratitude.

In "Joy Amidst the Sadness" I discus cancer patients of mine whose Gratitude for what they have in the most trying of situations, never fails to brighten my spirit. They are younger than I am and faced with a disease that is a serious threat to their life. Their young families are in turmoil because of the cancer. The pain and loss of vitality are gut-wrenching. Yet, so many of my patients are upbeat despite their trying situations. They concentrate on the doctors and nurses, their families and friends and on G-d's Grace.

May the Sustainer of Life grant you the wisdom and insight to always feel all the Blessings in your life.

Chapter 17
ALWAYS LOSING, ALWAYS HOPEFUL

As my time selling chemicals with the company I described with no love and affection in "Surviving and Thriving When the Worst Happens" was winding down, I ran into a real estate broker who had represented our family business for many years. He asked how I was doing and I responded that I was getting nowhere with trying to become a commercial real estate broker. He did what so many others have done for so many people: he made the suggestion that turned my business life around.

He said: try southern New Jersey.

I called several brokers and wound up going with the largest one in the market place. In April 2015, I will have been with NAI Mertz for more than twenty years. In all candor, I could write another book about the trials and tribulations of the business, as well as how long my commuting time, of give-or-take one hour and forty-five minutes, is a daily obstacle I have to overcome. If I had a shorter commute this book would have been published a few months earlier.

My Gratitude is that, after being in it nearly two decades, my biggest complaint is that I did not make the move earlier.

My family business was doomed from the start. That is easy to see now, but when you are making money it is very hard to see any unpleasant reality. There are many others who have experienced the same oversight but with often far more dire consequences than I felt. As one who has been in sales and general business for nearly forty years, I have heard too many life stories about how people got to where they are. They come from successful business owners and others with many achievements in their businesses or professions. One's path to accomplishments often has a foundation of failure. For some, it was not getting into the college of their choice. Others have been fired or laid off and then rebounded with resounding results. Yet others left an awful boss or owner to become their tormentor's greatest competition.

The message I took from my journey and others' is you never know what a setback will mean in the long term. It might just turn out to be a Blessing in disguise, so keep upbeat and hopeful. It is not easy but it can be done.

The suggestion my family friend made reminds me of another similar case in college where I was the one to make a remark that helped turned a friend's life around. When I learned about the ramifications of what I'd said, not only did I not remember it but I was totally shocked. During my freshman year, I had met an incredibly attractive female junior who hung out with many of my fraternity brothers. She had her pick of any guy she wanted. She not only was a knockout but was smart. For one midterm exam she forgot to buy the book or go to class. The only way she even knew there was an exam was a friend told her. Yet she aced it. As far as I know she never got any grade except for As. That young woman had everything, or so I thought.

In late spring 1970, the fraternity met as usual at a certain table to talk and eat. That time was truly my favorite part of the academic day. Yes, I was still not much of a student. On that particular day, for the only time I can remember in four years, it was just the two of us there: that wonderful young woman and I. At first, she did not realize I was there. Her face became very sad, something I had never seen on her. I asked her what was wrong, and she answered, "It is only a matter of time before I go down, too."

I looked at her in disbelief as she told me how her older sister, the pride of her family, had been in a car accident and was caught with drugs. Her mother's response was to have a nervous breakdown. Her father's response was to leave them both, saying he wanted nothing more to do with them. He did tell my friend not to worry, that there was plenty of money but that he was tired of fatherhood and needed to go somewhere without his family, friends or anyone else in his life. She concluded by saying, "Can't you see I am worthless? I have no chance to be anything."

I responded, "What does all this have to do with you?" She gave me a startled look so I added: "You have the money. Go see someone who can help you with all the *expletive* you have been through! Like a shrink."

I have no idea what happened next and frankly did not remember any of this conversation until I met her years later. One of my fraternity brothers lives in Philly threw a party and had invited her and her husband. When her husband and I were introduced, she gave me a huge hug as she told her husband: "This is the guy who told me to see the doctor who straightened me out after the accident."

He was exceedingly thankful for what I did for his wife. Bewildered I asked what she was talking about. She repeated my quote about seeing a psychologist. She went on to say she had to drop out of college for a year to get her act together, but she went back and became a very successful attorney. She and her husband had two great kids and were very happy. The therapist I suggested she see was the foundation for her recovery.

A few weeks later I remembered what had happened and why I made the remark about seeing a shrink. I had taken a psychology class and had heard how much money it costs to see one for a long period of time, but how helpful it can be. That is where I got the idea that came to me in an instant and was forgotten in an instant. I am deeply Grateful to learn that I had helped someone who seemed to have it all but was so troubled. It is amazing how we can help someone and not even know it.

What I took away from that wonderful story is to try to help people with any suggestions you think might help them. Never assume someone will know what you know. My friend, in all probability, had heard the same things about shrinks or psychiatrists. She was just too involved in her situation to think about it. I just happened to be in the right place at the right time for her. So make suggestions, but realize it is not up to you whether they take your advice. You may be totally right, but the decision lies only with the person you make the suggestion to.

As for the help I received to become a commercial real estate broker in Jersey, I am forever grateful for our family friend. I have to say the Almighty G-d works in mysterious ways and I believe He was at work with that suggestion. My work at this firm, in addition to bringing me a decent living (though nothing like the halcyon days of my family business), has allowed me to sprout my wings and do what I believe G-d intended me to do.

Our business functions like this: you work on a lot of deals that, if they all went through and you got paid a commission, your earnings would rival top sports or entertainment superstars. However, most of what you work on does not become a deal. That is the bad news. The good news is that you are always getting new opportunities.

Early on, I decided to focus on what I have going for me, not on what I lost. Remember, athletes are often the best brokers not because they are used to winning but because they are used to losing and bouncing back. With my early non-athletic career and my troubles with my number one sport, running, I feel I am a natural for the brokerage business!

In my family business I had always worried about what people would think of me. Employees, I thought, would naturally resent me because of my last name and seeming connections. In their eyes, I went into a business they were invested in and suddenly I am first in line to run the company, not because of my ability but my birth. That wasn't really what was going on in the company; it's just what I thought the employees believed about me.

Also, being from such a prominent family business in Philly, I was always concerned about protecting our assets and how I would be perceived in the community. After all, I had nothing to do with being a Kardon, that fell into my lap, so I always felt I had to prove myself worthy of it. Whenever anyone would meet me and learn my last name, I often wondered if they were impressed with me or was it my family name.

As a broker at a company with a different last name than mine, I had no such issues so I began to act like me. I joked and behaved in what I thought was a loveable and goofy way. I found being so at ease helped break the ice with clients and customers and was a rather enjoyable way to live. Turns out, people had a different and far better view of my goofiness.

I started to, and still do, hear how I am always in a good upbeat mood and spread sunshine. When I suffered a concussion in October 2012, I heard people at work missed my "happiness." They said it makes everyone feel good and upbeat.

Part of my personality has to do with me being very Grateful. Before I became a commercial real estate broker, I had endured probably five years of wondering what I would do for a living and had that absolutely awful, demeaning, albeit brief, sales job. Gail and I suffered a loss of status and economic security. There were so many times at the end of our family business that I felt very defeated.

Now I am doing something I enjoy that I get better at day by day, week by week and year by year. Almost immediately those weekends and nights of constant worry about my future and the fall of the family business were replaced by a sense of satisfaction that I found and used to reinvent myself. My father always lived under the cloud that he did not create the business and had wondered, as so many in other family businesses do, what would he inherit if the business was not there. I had self-worth. It felt greater than anything physical I could inherit.

I realized that I had lost my anger and replaced it with a sense of satisfaction when I thought about those in family businesses who considered me a leper due to the end of our business. I was worth something more than being in a family business. They still do not know how they would, or if they could, survive. I do.

One of the things I love about being a commercial real estate broker is that you have the freedom to do your business as you see fit. I was drawn to networking almost immediately. When you network, you go to various events hoping to meet people who need real estate in some way. You join organizations you think will help you get business. This activity allows me to meet a lot of people and work with them. It is good business and frankly, fun. When you go out for business having fun is vital. If you are not enjoying it, you will naturally skip events. The more you skip, the more distant you will feel from the group, and eventually you will give up.

The group I joined for the longest time was a group called TAP. While I am no longer a member, I did get some business from the group and discovered even more about how I can light up a room. Those awesome colleagues gave me nothing but positive feedback regarding how upbeat and inspiring I am. From that group I started to have a swagger whenever I would walk into a room of people. I could feel how my optimistic nature was giving me great confidence. I used to be a little nervous about going to any meeting. I no longer feel that way. Whenever a flash of dynamic personality is needed, I can feel myself being able to call upon it and find it.

Another business group is the Traffic Club of Philadelphia, founded in 1908, the year the Chicago Cubs and University of Pennsylvania football were World Series Champion and National Champion respectively. I worked my way through the ranks and became President in 2013-2014. It was an experience I cherished and love being a part of to this day. I have also joined other groups related to the Traffic Club of Philadelphia: NEARS and NARS both rail shipper groups. Recently I became involved in the Chamber of Commerce Southern NJ (CCSNJ), and the Society of Industrial and Office Realtors (SIOR) is another group I have become involved with. We are the most prestigious group of commercial real estate brokers in the world. I am in line to be President of the New Jersey chapter.

As my self-confidence grew, so did my success, not only in business but in many other areas of my life. There are many quotes about how life begins at an age ending in zero, or when the kids move out, and when the dog dies (sorry you dog lovers, it's not my saying). None really fit me. My life began when I walked into NAI Mertz Corporation on April 19, 1995.

Finding happiness in your work is not always easy. I found Gratitude to be a major part of not only getting through the day or week, but something that will make you more effective in whatever you do. I keep saying it because it's true: happier people tend to motivate others more. They will also have a greater chance of success in *any* kind of selling situation outside or inside the business. Think about it, what kind of person would you rather buy from or follow?

There are three areas I suggest you look at in your job, profession, or business to help you find Gratitude in your work.

- First, think about whom you work with. Through the years I have enjoyed the company of many people at work. Find out what interests you share with them. For me living in the Philadelphia area, the Philadelphia Eagles are a great unifier, as are many other teams whether professional, college or even high school. Sharing the experience of their wins and losses is fun and bonding. Yes, I intentionally included the losses. I admit I can enjoy losses because misery loves company. Besides, sports are a life-and-death situation that ultimately means nothing. I also enjoy talking about running with colleagues and congratulating each other on race completions. Many people enjoy sharing information about their kids, spouses, partners, life events, and on and on. The list is endless. Find what interests the people where you work, bond with them, get to know them. You will find Gratitude in how you enjoy your job much more.

- The second area to find Gratitude at work is the status it gives you. There are all too many stories about corporations letting go of baby-boomer employees who have had outstanding careers only to be replaced with people half their age at half the cost. During the time I looked for work, I felt how unpleasant it is to be "in transition." At networking events people tend to shy away from you and your confidence is shaken. Be Grateful you have a job, career, business whatever it is. Remember the power of that first question we ask each other in our society: *What do you do?*

- The third area is found in trying to take pride in what you do regardless of what it is. As a commercial real estate broker, I am the one who finds business homes for companies and organizations. I also arrange for leases or the selling of

133

someone's real estate. Someone who waits on tables can take pride in helping people enjoy their meal and those they are sharing it with. Nurses help people through illness and injury. Someone who repairs cars enables people to move around. Those who repair anything take great stress off their customers. Last winter we lost heat for two days. Trust me, having it back brought warmth to us and not just the temperature. We were back in our wonderful house! People who manage others and are fair and pleasant to work for, bring much happiness to those under them as well as to their loved ones. How many stories do you know of people with bad bosses taking it out on their families? Business owners provide jobs for people as well as the goods and services they provide to their customers.

May you be Blessed in whatever your main daily endeavor is with peace from excessive stress that hurts your quality of life, be among people you enjoy interacting with and whom you respect, find financial reward to support yourself and your family, and remember that when you are good to others, you serve the Sustainer of Life because all are created in His Image.

Chapter 18
JOY AMIDST THE SADNESS

On December 17, 2007, Jewish calendar 8 Tevet, 5676, I started being a Pastoral Care Visitor/Para Chaplain, or what I now refer to as a volunteer Chaplain, at the Hospital of the University of Pennsylvania (HUP). HUP is recognized in numerous rating systems as one of the top ten hospitals in the USA. Nearly every week I visit all the Jewish patients (give or take twenty-five) and cancer patients in Rhoads 3. On May 22, 2014, I was recognized with the Pastoral Care Department of HUP's Sprit of Caring Award. I have never earned a penny for my service, but I am paid handsomely.

A friend in the department asked me for one word that sums up what I do there. The answer was easy: *love.* I have such love for my patients as well as for those in the department. The folks who work there are all wonderful, warm and caring people. I am forever in their debt for accepting me as one of them since I am not ordained and am merely a volunteer. My patients inspire me in so many ways and make me deeply Grateful. They have also confirmed that it really does not matter what a person's race, religion, age, socio-economic status, sexual preference, nationality, etc. might be in order for that person to be a wonderful human being.

My patients have also given me a new love of people in general. That love has been the foundation for me to find fun in the mundane in life. I am known to high-five store clerks, clown around with strangers, and even dance to music in stores. The latter is dependent on me liking the music, of course.

My journey that called me to become a volunteer member of the clergy began in graduate school. At that time I was recently engaged to Gail and just starting an MBA (Master of Business Administration) at Temple University. The course work was boring to me as it was written to help future CEOs of Fortune 500 companies, not someone going into a family business infinitesimal compared to a Fortune 500. In Temple's defense, that is how business was taught back then. Temple's business school today, while not quite in the top ten, is close with a very dynamic curriculum designed for today's business world. The building I took classes in defines *state of the art*. I was there recently saying how I was born before my time.

In the program back then, you were allowed only two C grades. I came close to three my first year because I felt it more important to visit Gail's father during the day while everyone else was busy working. My reasoning was my homework could wait but not visiting that wonderful man who had produced the woman of my dreams.

There were a few times when my father's-in-law illness presented me with a situation that I will spare you the details of. Just know that each time I handled it without flinching or having it bother me beyond noticing the pain my father-in-law had. It helped us bond even more than we already were. My father-in-law had a great knack for joking around and I loved to oblige him. We had an enjoyable routine where I was the *pippac* (Yiddish for belly button) doctor. (I learned that from my brother-in-law, who had wished our *pippacs* good health one night. To this day I call him Pipaci). I would take his cigarettes, touch them with a lighter, and say he was fine. For me, I did that in part to wish his brain tumor away.

While visiting my father-in-law was a great thing to do, when I would get home, I found I had no interest in doing any studying. I was spent from being in the hospital for several hours. I was slated for three C's but somehow convinced a professor to give me a B in one of those courses.

After that semester my father-in-law was healthy enough to go to his store and I was able to concentrate on not getting another C, which I did succeed in doing. On graduation day, I was first to go downstairs and claim my diploma for fear they would wise up and take it away from me.

Several years later, we lost a dear friend to cancer. The last few weeks of her life was eased by hospice doing an amazing and supportive job. Our friend died in peace and the family, you could just tell, felt supported. Those wonderful hospice people helped not only the immediate family, but other family and friends as well.

Also coming to their aid was the amazing Rabbi of my synagogue at the time, First Rabbi at Har Zion who had replaced our longtime Rabbi who is now in Milwaukee (their gain, our loss). Between new Rabbi and hospice, along with my experience with my father-in-law, I knew this path was something I was meant to do.

A few short years later, when both Matt and Dan were out of the house, Jewish Family and Children's Service took out an ad in the Jewish Exponent (sometimes called the Explosion) for Para Chaplain Training. I followed up on it.

The training for Para Chaplain was phenomenal. The subject matter, classmates, and our leader were awesome. My mother became very active in asking me how it was going and kept asking if I really thought I could do it. She could not believe it was actually happening. The time was great for my mom and me to bond over my budding Ministry.

In BU I had flirted with the idea of becoming a Rabbi. No one really thought it was a great idea. As I would learn at the graduation of my daughter-in-law, that is the usual reaction to people of all faiths when they hear a family member is going into the clergy. At the time, the wife of a Rabbi, called Rebbetzen was expected to be an unpaid member of the synagogue staff and devote her life to supporting her husband and congregation. The same was true for Reverends and Pastors. Today the spouses (women clergy are common with the exception of Catholic, Orthodox Jews and Muslims to name a few) are no longer expected, for the most part, to do that. Gail wanted no part of such a life and I cannot blame her.

The more I thought about the arrangement I also knew I would not have been happy either. My mother blamed herself for me not doing it. To ease her conscience, I had made a joke with a lot of truth to it. I told her Dad had reminded me I would have to learn Hebrew and that with my academic history of struggling with languages, I decided it would be a better idea for me to keep to business.

Upon graduation, I asked the leader where I could go to volunteer. She told me I had to wait for hospice as my dad had passed too soon. She directed me to HUP where I went for a ten-week training session, going once a week. Again, I found love at first site. I was the only Jew in the class and still felt the love and respect. And I quickly found a new wonderful religion: Everyone's Religion. We all serve the Sustainer of Life by helping those created in His Image during very tough times in their lives.

Though I did violate one of the main rules about Pastoral Care at HUP. I converted an ordained Minister. She was a Dallas Cowboy fan and I converted her to being a Philadelphia Eagles fan.

About halfway through the course, I recognized the leader, the Administrative Chaplain, as someone who used to sell elevator services to my family business back when we had office buildings. We were both in a better place than we were when we first met. She has been such an amazing source of support and a great friend to me. Whenever I have any question or issues, she always knows what and how to say whatever I need. She always inspires me.

Another ordained Minister and part of the department is someone I had met outside of HUP at Philly Fit, to be discussed in "My Championship Team," when I became the walking coach. The picture of us after we did the Philly Marathon still stands in the Pastoral Care office. Walking with her was a treat. She had a way of praising G-d with everything she did. She also called me a member of the *G-d squad*.

The two heads of the department during my tenure are amazing people who believed in me. You cannot imagine how much that means to have such leaders call you one of their own. These friends and everyone else I meet in the Pastoral Care Department are full of such love, kindness and goodness.

Every time I go into the office and see anyone from the department I feel touched and inspired by their goodness. I am so deeply Grateful they actually consider me one of them. I said that already, but I say it again because it means so much to me. As one of the members of the department told me, "few can do what we do." What makes these folks so special is that they are paid so little and are so devoted because, as one of them told me, when it gets tough with any patient, you remember why you are there.

The nurses also deserve special mention. My main experience is with Rhoads 3 but it is very similar throughout HUP. Whenever we are in the same room as a nurse, they always thank us for being there. When we talk I can feel their gratitude for me. In addition to being skilled they, as a group, are truly caring people. They take their patients within their hearts and it shows. Two things I can always say and 99% of patients will agree with me on this: the food is terrible and the nurses are sensational.

The patients have touched me in a multitude of ways numerous times. I could not begin to think of all the people I have visited where I am amazed that my visit touches them! I am Grateful I have the privilege of being with them. Being in a big city hospital, there are a lot of people I meet with lesser means than I have. They are often younger and have had more tough times than I have many times over. Their condition is grave, and their problems like money and family issues the sickness (especially cancer) brings them are unbearable beyond anything I have ever experienced. Then they tell me how strong their faith is, and how Grateful they are. I say my prayer and I can feel how it touches them. Sometimes they cry. The Administrative Chaplain tells me tears are a gift from them and they honor me with their tears. I am moved by the thought.

At these times it is not just me uplifting my patients, my patients are raising me to heights I could have never imagined. I am a volunteer member of the clergy serving G-d. Just as G-d heals, I am healing. In saying my prayer I am doing one of Judaism's most scared mitzvahs (Commandments of G-d), the *bikkur cholim*, or visiting the sick. This mitzvah is held so high we are Blessed in the World to Come and on Earth. The best thing for me is I do not view this as something I am blessing anyone or serving G-d as much as G-d is blessing me with this holy work (words a Rabbi told me). Before and after I start my visits I thank Him for how He is blessing me with this mitzvah. When I miss visits due to illness or other reasons (very rare) I feel like it is me missing out on something.

There is also the challenge my patients present to me. Even though I call myself Attitude of Gratitude, I never feel I have enough. When you see people with so much less than you past, present and future, you never feel you are Grateful enough for all you have. I have my health they do not. I am financially secure as long as Gail and I can work. My patients sometimes have only a few visitors because their families need to work to support them, which makes the patients feel isolated. I am always so Blessed to be spending time with so many people I care deeply about and enjoy being around.

Before and after a typical visit, I will work out and sometimes will do a half-marathon race or the like. Yet those patients are lucky to walk around the hall, which is only one-seventeenth of a mile long. They have very little control over their life while staying in the hospital. I am free to come and go as I please. They, in so many ways, have lost all dignity with what must be done to them in a hospital. I very much have my dignity except with endurance events where modesty always is stripped away. Of course, it is my choice and if you ask any endurance athlete about it, and we share a laugh or more. My patients are not laughing about their situation.

The bottom line for me is this: I am on the right side of the bed. No matter how sad the room, once I leave it, I am gone. That is not callous; it is why strangers are needed for the job. We can be very sympathetic but not emotionally involved. If we were, no one would be able to handle it. Perhaps the best benefit to me is that the time I spend on self-pity is even less than I ever spent before, and that thought brings me a lot of true joy.

There are a few cases I want to share with you that have been true blessings in my life. The first is when a Protestant Pastor wanted to see me on his last day to say a prayer to me for being such a friend and inspiration to me. He was also one of the warmest loving people I have ever met. The love his wife and daughters had for him warmed the room and I felt so fortunate to have known him.

There was also a woman with a loving family whose eyes lit up whenever I walked in the room. Their gratitude for my prayer and presence touched me deeply.

There have been many who tell me my prayer is so sincere, they can feel it. Many have also said they want to do what I am doing when they get better. Recently that happened when the husband of a patient asked to do the Challah Delivery (to be discussed below). He now does this and we have become friends.

Recently a dear friend told me he wants to do what I do. He will be great at it and I look forward to sharing our holy work together.

Another Orthodox woman who also visits the sick is getting great insight into what her patients are going through. As she explained, patients perform a function for us, the volunteer visitors, by being sick.

There was a man in his early forties who lost his legs in a motorcycle accident that subsequently caused his wife to leave him. A very short time later he came down with terminal cancer. He could do nothing except help the kids in the neighborhood with their homework. The cards in his room showed how someone with no legs and debilitating terminal cancer could still inspire so many.

And one day a nurse handed me a note from a patient's spouse thanking me for my prayer for their beloved. It was the last words they ever heard with their eyes open.

My visits sometimes have very happy endings. There was a young woman in her late teens who had a minimum of ten visitors every visit until the last one. She was not in when I stopped by one day, only her parents were there. They were cleaning up and getting ready to take her home. They were happy to see me and to thank me. They told me her bone marrow transplant was working. She would be OK. Bone marrow transplants were pioneered by a research team who got early seed money from American Cancer Society (ACS). In the coming chapters my involvement with ACS will be gone over in detail so you will understand then why that comment made me so happy.

Another man never had any evidence of anyone visiting him. He had a painful looking tube and could only nod at me when I asked if I could say a prayer. On my last visit with him, he could speak and was obviously going to be fine. He asked me for a prayer to give him strength for all the people who wanted to see him when he got home. His heartfelt *thank you* brought tears to me.

A few times my prayer (shown below) helped patients and their loved ones break the tension. A part of my prayer deals with loved ones and coming together to support each other. While most of the time I do not get to go into much detail regarding my patients' lives, there have been times I have been Blessed to help people in extraordinary situations. A terminally ill patient was estranged with her sibling. After dealing with her issues of facing death, we discussed the pain my patient felt. I suggested she try to make contact. They did and I got to see them together the next week. That visit was short but oh, so sweet. They were laughing and joking around.

Another sibling relationship meant I had to guide them to the conclusion that the relationship could not be repaired by my patient. There was child abuse involved and my patient wanted to shield his sibling from it. The sibling obviously had too much guilt to deal with to have a relationship. My patient was grateful for me for helping him realize that.

One of the great rewards to me during my visits is my ability to connect with fellow Jews as well as those of other faiths. In my Ministry I have learned that we are truly created in the image of G-d. Acknowledging that made me realize that I like people and find them fascinating. Now, in the back of my mind, whenever I see a stranger, instead of thinking how awful they must be because they are different from me, I wonder what makes them special.

I do not like to watch the news because it emphasizes the worst in people. I would rather see the best in people. I am far from naïve to believe that there are no evil people or groups out there. I know there are people who hate me simply because I am a Jew and American. While I do not ignore that fact, I would rather think about all the good I have seen and, G-d willing, will continue to see in human beings, again Created in the image of the Almighty.

There are two things I have learned about doing Pastoral Care I want to give you to. First, everyone always asks: "what do I say to someone who experienced a loss or serious injury of a loved one?"

My answer is not meant to be flippant but, why do you want to be a chatterbox? In the case of visiting or calling someone, your presence speaks volumes. By being there you show you care.

At a house of mourning I told the son, "I'm sorry for your loss." His eyes lit up and he said "thank you." So many asked how he was doing. In our society today those words seem to be accepted as appropriate. In the case of the hospital or home visit, say something like, *I'm thinking of you* or ask *Can I get you anything?* The next words of your conversation should come from the person you are visiting. Everyone handles the situation differently. Just listen. Some will want to discuss their loved one. Others may want to talk about something mundane to get their mind off of the sadness. Let them guide you.

The second thing I learned and want to share is a great term: Reverent Acknowledgement. That simply means recognize the pain someone is in. If they say, for instance, how uncomfortable they are, tell them you can see how difficult it must be for them. People in pain need to know that those around them empathize with them and what better way than to say so?

During a December visit to a seventy-one-year-old Jewish woman, I came up with the idea for a Challah Delivery program. Challah is a twisted bread traditionally served at Friday night dinners to celebrate the start of the Sabbath. She was sharing a room with someone who had many visitors. Her side had no evidence of any visitors. Christmas ornaments were all around the hospital.

Her eyes lit up when I told her I was a Jewish Pastoral Care visitor. With the joint effort of the Golden Slipper Club and Jewish Family and Children Service, we now have a Challah Delivery just before the Sabbath or Shabbos. I learned from that woman how important it is to patients to bring them *anything* to give comfort or remind them of the outside. Many patients bring their own blankets or even stuffed animals. That is not childish but just an attempt to get some solace during a difficult time.

And finally, here is the basic prayer I use for my patients.

G-d, I ask that it be Thy Will that my patients

Have a full and complete healing of both body and mind.
At this time Bless all my patient's loved ones
So that everyone will know what to give each
Other to get through this time,
And maintain and sustain each other and be strong together.

Spread over my patient Your Sheltering and Loving Presence
To protect them and grant them peace and comfort
When they call upon You.
May they always feel that Sheltering and Loving Presence.

Grant them Your Spirit
So they have the insight, wisdom, strength and courage
To know Thy Will and
Perform Thy Will
And get through this time.
And be with them all now and always.

Amen.

Chapter 19
THE BIG RIDE

You may recall that in May of 2000, a family friend and I discussed cycling. I was doing ten- to fifteen-mile rides in the neighborhood. He discussed doing the American Cancer Society (ACS) Bike-a-Thon every year. That ride, at that time, was a sixty-one mile trek that benefits the ACS. With all the history of cancer in my family at an early age, along with Gail's father, and so many other loved ones of mine and people I care about, I was drawn to the cause right away. The challenge was also enticing.

Matt was by my side during this discussion and I could feel him getting excited about it, too. Unfortunately we couldn't do the ride in 2000, because we already had a wonderful family wedding planned that weekend. So we decided 2001 would be the year.

As I discussed earlier, Matt and I accomplished three long training rides so we felt we were ready for that auspicious day: July 15, 2001. At the suggestion of the family friend we found a team captained by someone who wound up changing my life (again!).

The night of July 14, 2001, Matt and I went to the team pre-ride dinner. We were both nervous and excited. The dinner was very inspiring (although it didn't have the same impact as the one we subsequently went to in 2002).

We woke up just after three o'clock in the morning on Ride Day and ate a breakfast consisting of a bowl of oatmeal and a banana. Gail drove us to the team meeting point where our captain was happy to see us. He gave us instructions and then we were off to the start line.

At the line, our captain recited the instructions to more than 3,500 riders. He also reminded everyone why we were riding. I could feel the emotions around us as people remembered loved ones lost to the disease. Others riding were inspired survivors (very uplifting to see them and their *in your face cancer!* attitude). And there were still others riding to support a loved one currently fighting the disease. Above all else I could sense the power of so many people coming together to rid humanity of the scourge called cancer. I was also very impressed with our captain. There was just something very special about him.

The ride started by crossing the Ben Franklin Bridge. I love driving over it on my way to work so it was amazing for me to be there with no cars, just bikes. I got the chance to love the bridge up close and personal, which made me think of my father. I remembered him telling me how, when he was four years old, the day before they opened the bridge to cars, everyone was allowed to walk it.

The route was crowded with fast riders passing us as well as with slower riders we had to pass. After the rest stop halfway there, Matt wanted to ride side by side with me for the remainder of the race. We had such joy together.

When we were five miles from the endpoint, we decided to pass up the last rest stop and just go for it. We crossed the finish line together and gave each other a big hug of triumph. Leann Womack was singing, "I Hope You Dance" on the loudspeaker. I shed some happy tears and the song became the first of so many to remind me of all the endurance events I am so Blessed to be able to do. Matt and Dan both panned the song, which just makes me laugh about the difference in our generations.

The next year when we went to the team dinner, I began my journey as a volunteer with ACS that continues to this day, growing stronger and stronger. We sat with the ACS staff partner in charge of the event. She and her husband were enjoyable to sit with, making the dinner even more enjoyable. She told us that our team captain, in addition to forming a strong team that is usually the biggest fund raiser, chaired the whole event.

The next day was full of problems. The bananas were green and it rained.

A few days later, the staff partner wrote a contrite letter. I left a voicemail message of support and raved how my son and I love Bike-a-Thon. She called me back and asked me to join the committee. I said that if Matt wanted me to, I would. He was very excited and went with me to the next meeting on November 18, 2002. Wanting to impress Matt, I spoke up quite a bit at the meeting. The Committee response was: "Great! You can co-chair whatever committee they put me on." As I left, some veterans told me, "Welcome aboard." Matt would come to one or two more meetings and then leave. I have been indebted to him ever since.

Before joining Bike-a-Thon (BAT), I had been on many other committees and involved with several causes. When the kids came along and finances became an issue, I withdrew so BAT was like a revival for me. Thanks to ACS, it was also something of a coming-out party.

I have always been passionate and enthusiastic about what and who I like. What I learned at ACS was that what I thought was loveable goofiness in myself, was something that could actually inspire people and make them feel better about themselves. It seemed whenever I would get excited about something, I would be met by smiles of approval. What made it all even more special was the fact that the family business was long gone. No one was welcoming me because my name was Kardon but because I was Roy. It felt great. For the first time in my life I discovered the best part of me. ACS, is a volunteer-driven organization that embraced me as I was embracing them.

There is much I love about ACS. The staff partners and volunteers are some of the most wonderful people I have ever met in my life. The camaraderie and support we give each other brings me such joy and happiness. I feel so Blessed to have fellow volunteers and staff partners in my life. By the time of my writing this now, I am a leader at ACS, having won the Volunteer Achievement Award and the Distinguished Service Award.

The mission of the ACS is also something that gives me such pride. I have met a few people who see the ACS on my shirt and say, "thank you." Some have told me how they appreciate the day-to-day things ACS does, like arrange for rides to treatment or self-help groups. One person said, "I was scared when I got my diagnosis and needed to talk to someone at three in the morning. Your hotline had the most wonderful person answer the phone when I called. They were so helpful and supportive."

A couple of folks who actually worked for other cancer groups told me they realized the ACS were the ones always involved in every initiative to help, no matter who originates or runs it. In Chicago, I ran into a wonderful couple who told me our money helped save their daughter who happens to be a doctor. She knew how our early seed money made the difference in timing that ultimately saved her life.

Of course as a Volunteer Chaplain I have seen numerous patients undergo chemotherapy that, while painful has saved many lives. And it was ACS seed money that helped make that breakthrough possible.

The personal connection with what ACS does is as close as it can get to me since it involves the love of my life, my wife, and soul mate, Gail. On February 27, 2004, a mammogram showed that Gail had breast cancer. The next couple of weeks were very tense because we did not know the extent of the cancer. The weekend before meeting with the doctor, Gail had asked me to do some research to prepare for that doctor meeting.

The ACS website was amazing. Every type of cancer was there. I quickly found all I needed and then tried to find more on the internet but no one had any more to offer. Thanks to the mammogram, Gail's cancer was caught in time. Since then, she has told two friends to get the exam done. It ended up very likely saving their lives. I know there are studies saying mammograms do not work or whatever. But with all due respect, I totally disagree. And not surprisingly mammograms, were pioneered in part with ACS seed money.

The BAT ride in 2003 was the first with me being on the committee. It was a sensation. I rode without Matt for the first time but found many others along the route I knew. Soon I discovered the joy of talking to many strangers who, for a moment, became best friends. I felt such pride in being part of that event. At the same time, I was pleasantly surprised by how much was done to make the day possible that I never knew about. I still feel that way about the ride and other ACS endeavors. And love that feeling. Being part of something bigger than you, makes you feel so much bigger where it counts: in how happy you are and how good you feel about yourself and others.

Our team captain quickly became my hero. His selfless devotion to the fight was what I could only ever dream of doing. But he made it seem so possible to do yet more. He would step aside from being chair a few years later. The leadership structure remained with two co-chairs and me, in many ways their deputy or assistant. Both of them were wonderful and dedicated leaders who continued my captains' fine leadership.

My captain remained very active by having a top fund-raising team and raising so much money himself. I became very comfortable with the new leadership structure until I went to a reception for one of our teams in March 2008. One of the co-chairs announced he was stepping down and said the most terrifying, life-changing words: "Meet my replacement, Roy Kardon." He must have noticed the shock on my face because he added something about maybe I had not "received the memo."

Although I had plenty of opportunity to get out of situation, I did not take it. I had three reasons for not doing so. First, my fellow co-chair and staff partner were such a pleasure to be around. In addition, they are incredibly competent and dedicated. The two years, 2009 and 2010, that I had with them are ones I will always cherish. I will always consider that time to be among the most pleasant ones in my life. I am happy to still be in contact with both of them.

A second reason I followed through as co-chair was because of my love for ACS and its mission. Yes, it would be easy to do what I had been doing, but then I would have ignored a need ACS had at the time.

The third reason is that I wanted to be in the footsteps of my amazing captain. One of the two happiest BAT moments for me was in 2009 when I arrived in our team tent to cheers led by my captain. The other was seeing friends of mine take over the leadership and relish the success on ride day.

In 2010, I would step down as co-chair to become chair of DetermiNation. That move actually started with an idea from the first ever BAT pre-ride on June 16, 2006. That day, one of the co-chairs and I were doing the ride just to make sure the route was OK for the big ride. At one point I suddenly found myself off road and unable to stop. I tried to get back onto the road but was thrown off my bike and landed in the street. Every car driver who saw it happen, stopped to ask how I was.

The co-chair changed my flat tire and asked if I was OK or if I needed to be picked up by one of our staff partners supporting us. I was dazed for about a minute from the crash but I decided to try continuing on anyway and was OK riding the final forty-nine miles. At the end of the ride they told me that my helmet was cracked. I also had a nasty gash at the point of impact. So for those of you out there who have heard my lecture on wearing helmets, that is where it comes from.

A couple days later an X-ray showed I also had a broken rib. I was told to stay away from outside bike riding but that I could use my indoor machine and walk all I wanted to. I love outside sports and really missed not riding. Walking got me through it and soon became my next number-one passion, which would, in turn, lead me to DetermiNation.

DetermiNation is an American Cancer Society program where we support endurance event participants with training, emotional support, and by providing an amazing tent for the start and finish of our athletes' life-enhancing day.

To this day I remain on the BAT committee and, as stated above, love seeing friends take over leadership positions and grow the event that changed and enhanced my life. The people involved are such wonderful people who give so much time and money to support a cause bigger than all of us. BAT is where I discovered that I am a leader who has "infectious enthusiasm." I have been called "an inspiration" and "the most selfless person." None of the foregoing are my words, they're just what I've been told.

I am forever in debt to ACS for helping me discover the best in me and showing me the best in others

I am not the only person to have found such beauty and happiness

150

in volunteering. There are many uplifting quotes about it and I love the poem titled, "You only get to keep what you give away." Giving of yourself elevates you in every way.

Finding the right opportunity is not always as easy as it would seem, though. As one who has been through many volunteer experiences, I advise you to follow your heart and look at the people involved. Is it a cause that pulls at your heart strings? Does the prospect of success of the cause mean something to you? Will you get emotionally involved with it? As to the people, the questions to ask yourself are simple. Do you want to spend time with them? Could they become your friends? Are they fun to be around?

You must also, in a very matter-of-fact way, analyze whether it is a good fit for you. Are the activities they do something you will enjoy? For instance, I love endurance sports so working with ACS to create endurance events works for me. If you love a cultural activity and that is what the volunteer work involves, that could work for you. If you love animals, working around saving them would be good for you.

Unfortunately, I conclude this chapter on a profoundly sad note. Late in the summer of 2013, my captain and his wonderful wife went out for a bike ride. He suffered a heart attack and in spite of heroic efforts from bystanders, he was unable to be revived. He was only fifty-nine.

One of the things I remember hearing in synagogue during the weekly services at Main Line Reform Temple where I grew up is: "They shall be remembered in the acts of goodness they performed." My captain changed my life. Without him I would not have joined the BAT committee and discovered so many wonderful qualities I never knew I had. I also would not have been touched by his and so many others with selfless devotion to a cause bigger than themselves. He lives on in me and in so many others graced to have known him.

May all your volunteer and selfless endeavors bring you closer to the Sustainer of life and those created in His Image. As you give of your time and/or money, may you feel the joy of your life touching others. May your loved ones share in the happiness and satisfaction you receive.

Chapter 20
My Championship Team

The theme song I adopted for Bike-a-Thon (BAT), "I Hope You Dance" by Leann Womack, contains some beautiful lyrics that are similar to Alexander Graham Bell's famous quote: *When one door closes, another opens; but we often look so long and so regretfully upon the closed door that we do not see the one which has opened for us.* In the summer of 2006 I was faced with a closed door. I was unable to ride because of the rib injury I had sustained.

The irony is we had rented a place at the shore, the place where my love of cycling had started. I had to do quite a bit of walking, which turned into yet another exercise love affair that I enjoy to this day. Walking you can do just about anywhere anytime, even in bad weather if you have the appropriate clothing.

That summer I frequently took long walks along the boardwalk in Atlantic City and Ventnor. The problem was there was not an event or a way to challenge myself the way BAT did. I did an AIDS walk in 2007 around the West (Martin Luther King) River Drive and East (Kelly) River Drive in Philadelphia, which consisted of 8.4 miles. It was lovely, but I felt a little out of place with no one trying to go fast.

In December of 2007, I was getting ready to start my Pastoral Care visits at HUP. It was also the middle of the holiday season with its numerous parties. While I love the season I do realize the main holiday is Christmas, something that, as a Jew I do not observe. I have no problem with the holiday, though, and truly enjoy so many other people being so happy. I love the message of *Peace on Earth* and what one amazing Priest at a luncheon called this season: The Season

152

of Light. I thought it was fantastic how he could bring together both celebrations: Christmas and Chanukah.

Every year I go to a Chanukah party, and 2007 was no different. The group that held it was the Jewish Business Network (JBN). On that amazing night I walked in and saw a friend I had not seen in a couple years. We had tried to do business together but nothing came from it. She had a model-like figure so when she told me she had a baby who was just eight months old, I had to ask how she stayed in shape. She said she walked in running races. That night I went home and registered for the 2008 Blue Cross Broad Street Run to take place on May 4, 2008. It is a ten-mile race, the largest ten-miler in the USA.

I built up my walking with one big walk each week, along with several shorter ones. That's how training programs work for those kinds of races. Somehow I figured that out before learning that that is how it was done. Seemed to me, it was meant to be.

The training was a true delight. I did a couple of ten-mile training walks and was totally ready to finish a race. I had waited thirty-three years from my first run (not organized but still a run to me) on May 20, 1975, of 3.9 miles, to do another race. On race day, I saw the *thirty-three years* all over. Actually it was sixteen days short of thirty-three years, but I loved the idea of thirty-three years. I called the day a coronation.

I knew I could do it. And finally being part of a running race was a dream that I had thought would never come true. While I was not formally a runner, no one ever said or acted like I was not part of any race. As I mentioned before, the running community is a very supportive, welcoming and warm group. There had been countless times when I was cheered on at the end of a race by runners who finished an hour or more before me. They not only cheered but also they would look at their watch and then give me such a look of respect for being out there so long. Frank Shorter, one of the greatest long distance runners ever, has a quote about how much he respects people like me doing six-hour marathons.

On May 4, 2008, I went with a friend from work and finished the race easily averaging 13-minute-42-second miles. Due to traffic from a Phillies game nearby, I was stuck afterward in a parking lot for forty-five minutes but I loved it. I was in that good of a mood.

153

I was also so Grateful to the Almighty for blessing me with that gift after thirty-three years. I welled up with tears as I walked back to my car. In September of that year, with my friend who told me about walking, I finished my first-half marathon, the Philadelphia Distance Run, now a Rock 'n Roll event.

We planned to do the Philadelphia Half-Marathon together but she had to pull out that day. With maybe one percent of the race running, I broke three hours. When I went immediately afterward to pick up something for Gail, I was still in my uniform and realized people were looking at me. Gail called while I was still out to ask how I did. As I told her, I could feel more admiration come my way.

In movies you always seem to have a scene where the future is shown to you. That happened to me that day. The Philadelphia Half-Marathon also had a Full Marathon run at the same time. Remember earlier when I mentioned seeing a couple from a YouTube video embrace after that run? They were celebrating doing the full marathon. As I watched them I said to myself *Forget it! A half is enough.* But I knew in the back of my mind that when the weather got warmer, I would be trying to do my first marathon. It would be thirty-eight years after I had started to run back in Boston.

My first goal during the winter months was to locate a group that I could train with. I did not consciously think about a marathon but that really was why I was doing it. Our mind plays great tricks on us. I found plenty of running groups but no mention of walking at all. There were walking groups for single, gay/lesbian or women. While I was happy to see those groups bonding, it did not help me at all. My friend who got me into it became very busy with a small child and starting a business.

As soon as I could, I registered for the Blue Cross Broad Street Run. One night I looked at the list of groups that would be at the expo and found a one called Philly Fit, part of USA Fit. They advertised for walkers also as full members of the group. They did not start training until the second Saturday in May but were going to be at the expo.

At the expo, I picked up my packet and headed over to their table. I asked them if the training would interfere with the other sports I did, especially cycling and swimming. Whoever it was said plenty of members did multiple sports. I got the email of the organizer and emailed her the question: "Could they really train me to walk a marathon and have fun doing it?" She replied and told me I would have to provide the fun but definitely, yes, they could train me. Reading between the lines of the email, I felt confident that was the group for me.

I loved it from day one. Everyone was so incredibly nice, welcoming and supportive. I was quickly made to feel that I was one of the team and not to concern myself about the fact that most were runners and I was a walker. Armed with what ACS had taught me about my exuberance, I started to cheer everyone as we would pass each other during the first run/walk. I then became a regular writer on our closed website, always trying to encourage people on our team. The end result was I found myself to be an inspirational part of a team that was helping me do a marathon, something that had eluded and frustrated me for thirty-eight years. That kind of thing is not supposed to happen when you are fifty-eight, but I kept moving quickly and in what seem to be an unstoppable manner in order to finish a marathon.

The year 2009 was also when Attitude of Gratitude took hold for me. I had never run a race without my byline. The name for me came in the spring of 2009 at the Golden Slipper Club & Charities Annual Model Seder. We have about 500 seniors come to that annual event. I always helped our guests off the bus and noticed that there was one bus that night where it seemed everyone was incredibly slow and struggling. The seniors were showing their physical age but not spirit. They were joking around as they fought to get off that bus with their limitations. One apologized to me, and I said with fervor, "I love your attitude." They responded, "We have an Attitude of Gratitude." That night for $35.43 I bought my first shirt on line with those words.

The Blue Cross Broad Street Run had a very funny footnote to it. Numerous people came up to me asking if, I was a friend of Bill. On maybe the tenth such interaction, I replied with, "This Bill must be quite a guy." The respondent said with deep conviction, "He sure is."

Turns out Bill, is Bill Anderson, the founder of Alcoholics Anonymous, someone else who used the phrase *Attitude of Gratitude*.

When I learned that, I became very proud to share one of that super human being's sayings.

On October 16, 2009, I decided to try a half-marathon because the timing did not work for my local race: the Philadelphia Distance Run was held on Rosh Hashanah. I chose to go down to Baltimore to do the 2009 Baltimore Half-Marathon instead. It was an incredible twenty hours or so out of my life.

The moment I checked into the hotel and picked up my packet, I began talking to other participants and delighted in everyone wishing me good luck. I was an out-of-town athlete, just like the pros. I found a perfect restaurant from which to take dinner back to the hotel. The race started at nine-thirty, so I had a chance to watch on TV the start of the Marathon and walk around and see the sights and sounds first.

During the race, I looked for a friend from Philly Fit, but did not find him until the race started. He was ten feet away from me but no way would we connect. We did not even see each other at the end because it was still too crowded. It would have been special seeing him. He was my walking coach and the only walker who I know who is faster than I am. He had given me great pointers, including when registering for the NYC Marathon to do it early and get enough rejections so that I could get in automatically for 2013.

Other than not seeing my friend it was a perfect race. I finished with 12-minute-11-second miles beating out one-sixth of all participants. I passed numerous runners and to cheer them up I clowned around with them. One group did say: "He is over the top" when I thanked a police officer. It was a sign of true respect, so I thought. If they wanted to catch me, they could not in spite of the fact that they were running.

What a fabulous day, except for one little pain climbing up a hill. It was around mile seven or eight and did not seem like a lot. The final mile they had people giving out gummy bears saying, *Gummy bears will take you there.* For the first time in my racing career, I had to use made up "anger" to get me through. I told myself they were insulting me by thinking I needed sugar. But I had the heart of an athlete so long

156

denied being a part of these events that nothing would have stopped me. I kept screaming to myself, *Heart will get me there!* I did that at the same time that I thanked the holders of the gummy bears for helping out with a smile.

A couple weeks later we did our final long training run/walk of twenty-one miles. It was not my day. I struggled and had that same pain in my left big toe. I went to the doctor and was quickly diagnosed with sesamoiditis. The doctor put me into an elastic cast to immobilize the muscle and hopefully allow me to go on the November 22, 2009, Philadelphia Marathon. He told me to ride my bike machine and that I would be OK once my toe healed. The Tuesday before the Marathon I went to him all nervous. The appointment was quick and simple and I was cleared to go after my first marathon in my life.

Throughout the year I had been inspiring people. One friend even called me Sunshine.

When I had posted to the group that I was questionable, I had received such touching responses like "Roy, you were the one who always motivated me."

On that amazing day I was paid back. As I got to the parking lot I played songs from the Rocky movies, including, "Gonna Fly Now" and "Going the Distance." On the later song I broke down and cried thanking G-d, as I knew that whatever would happen that day I was going to do a marathon. I walked to the Rocky Statue at the Philadelphia Museum of Art and saw my team mates. They all hugged me. That was quite a moment. Since I really never got the chance to talk during training walk/runs and was not there for the Philadelphia Distance Run, our only contact was cheering each other on and always with me starting it.

I could never tell those wonderful people how much it meant to me that they hugged me so. We all talked and I felt very calm, confident and ready. But my success at Baltimore got me off to a rough start. I thought I was faster than I was and for the first mile everyone was passing me. As I went by the Four Seasons Hotel, I wished I was still sleeping and about to enjoy a sumptuous brunch.

Once again my team was there for me. As I passed the one mile marker, I noticed my time was 12-minutes-45-seconds a very good time. At that moment two team mates passed me saying, "Go Roy." A couple feet down the road there was an ACS staff partner I would meet for the first time. I hugged her and was ready to get this done. Around mile seven, my walker friend caught up with me. It was as always great to see him. We went to the side to make our own bathroom (very common in running races even with women) as his wife and sister-in-law shouted, "We have your numbers you are busted!" What a great laugh. A friend from Philly Fit took my picture with me smiling and the caption reading "Roy, doing his first marathon happy as always."

The happiness would soon turn as it inevitably does in marathons to pain. At the thirteen-mile mark going off to the right means you're doing half, to the left is mile fourteen, you're doing the full. The second half was brutal. I was exhausted and struggling. I kept thinking I had a blister, which fortunately was false. My pain grew and grew until I reached mile twenty-five and a friend from Philly Fit, who was cheering us on, came up to me hugging me and smiling, telling me I had done it.

Now you must remember the mind is not all coherent after twenty-five miles, which had taken me over five-and-a-half hours to do at that point. My imagination made for one phenomenal finish. First I said to the pain, "It's over I win now go away." Pain responded, "I will leave you on the course but I will be cheering you the whole way in. I am so proud of you I hope you will do this again, so we can have another battle." I said to pain, "You know I will and pain I love you." Pain said, "I love you too." As the finish line came closer I heard the announcer say, "Thirty-eight years of defeat and frustration are ending. Let the celebration begin. Roy Kardon you are a marathoner a marathon finisher."

I quickly found some team mates including my friend. We posed for a picture and my body made clear I needed to go to my car, sit down and drink some water. We congratulated everybody and off I went. An officer saw my Attitude of Gratitude shirt and my age and said to me, "G-d Bless you sir." I responded "G-d Bless you officer."

At home my Dan had several friends over to watch the Eagles game.

It was the only time he let me fall asleep and not wake me. His friends had such respect for me. It felt great. I limped around that Sunday and Monday until I got on my bike machine and rode without resistance for maybe a half hour. From that point on, I was fine.

All those years of wishing I was on a team had come true for me in 2009. I would go on to coach the walkers for two years before commitments and races would take me away from coaching but not the group. Unfortunately, I work a great distance from where the group does many week night runs. With our place at the shore I am also there rather than local, when they do some riding.

I am still a part of the group. Although Philly Fit is no more, several of us are now part of the Jeff Galloway Training group. It is so awesome to be with them again and the non-Philly Fit members are equally as wonderful human beings. They are so supportive of everyone. I look forward to continuing to be with this championship team of athletes and people.

For all the emphasis on physical fitness in our society, there are still so many who have not added this life enhancing activity on a consistent basis. What I learned from Philly Fit is the power of running in a group. This year I did an 8.8 mile run called the Hot Foot. As I ran passed a young woman, she saw my *Chicago 2014 Marathon* tagline and said with admiration, "You did a marathon." I looked for her at the end of the race but did not find her. I wanted so much to tell her that if she could do 8.8 she could do 26.2, the marathon distance.

Training for a marathon is like playing football. You keep in shape during the week and do a long run on the week end. The run will be exhilarating and you will need time to recover just like a football game. When you do it in a group, you will typically find a group doing your speed. They will become your main training partners. If you live or work near each other, you will often do some training during the week, too.

Women seem to gravitate toward training in groups. My observation is threefold. Many women in training groups have no experience on being on a team and they love this support. Women are obviously more vulnerable running alone. And finally, women

159

seem to enjoy being part of a group more so than men in a general sense. This does not mean men do not benefit, but women seem to benefit more.

Another benefit from groups is the support on race day and in your life in general. I am always amazed at how upbeat I feel after any communication with a team mate whether it be in person or on Facebook. Race day is always very crowded. Being with someone else feels as if you have your fans and special team mates there just for you.

Please remember that while I refer to running, I also mean walking. Just about any running store will cater to walkers as though they were runners. I mentioned running because that is what races are known as and referred to. But make no mistake about it walkers, you are in every way a part of the running scene.

And a special note to those of you who may weigh more than the average and are self-conscious about it: one of the most inspiring things I see in this sport and in triathlons as well, is the welcome you will receive. There is something so uplifting about seeing someone tackle any race as part of trying to improve their health and appearance. There are so many instances of weight-challenged people finishing a race and telling others about their journey. It never fails to stir up the pride we have for being part of the same race as these fellow athletes. We know how much it means to you and we are there to share in your joy. May you be Blessed as you start your journey.

Finding groups can be done by going to Google online, with charities like American Cancer Society (to be discussed in next chapter), Meet up, through running stores, etc. Come to the group expecting your life to be enhanced and transformed. Races, organized rides, and triathlons, for me has been the foundation of so much personal growth and joy in my life. May you be Blessed as you go forward and HAVE FUN. GET IT DONE.

Chapter 21
THE GREATEST NATION

Shortly before Bike-a-Thon in 2010, my staff partner told me about a new initiative within ACS called DetermiNation (DNation). It is an endurance sports initiative where we support, train and give our athletes an incredible race weekend for an event not run by ACS.

The main events we do this for are the Blue Cross Broad Street Run and the Gore Tex Philadelphia Full- and Half-Marathon. I went to a couple meetings and loved the people. Unfortunately, there were very few of them. I fell in love with the program though and after being involved in both BAT and DNation, I knew I would eventually be asked to take on a larger role with DNation. Sure enough, my staff partner and very close friend talked to me about it just around the time I could see it coming.

I had been with BAT for nearly eight years and was enjoying being co-chair. DNation was definitely still a work in progress. My friend always says, "G-d has a plan." I love that saying as it's another way to say G-d's Will. As we spoke about my situation, two things were very clear: there were plenty of people to take my place at BAT and DNation in its infancy needed to add people to make it a success. I asked my friend and staff partner what was in the best interests of ACS and answered the question myself. The one condition I had was that I would remain on the BAT committee. I am still to this day and expect to remain a part of the event that changed my life and honors the memory of my captain.

Even though it was a struggle at first for us, we had one major thing going: in nearly every instance when someone gave us a chance to show what we had to offer, they loved us and we loved them. The group is so welcoming and encouraging. Just like BAT, people love to do things to make us better. ACS seems to have that effect on people by bringing out the best in them. As much as I was upset to lose my staff partner (but not our friendship), I have to say I have amazing staff partners at DNation. Our committee has grown from about three to four members to around twenty-five. And we keep having new people show up and get involved.

For the Blue Cross Broad Street Run, we had close to 825 runners, and I believe in a couple years we will hit the $1,000,000 mark, net. Best of all is that I am no longer chair but co-chair, a great testament as to how we have grown and blossomed. My co-chair is both an amazing athlete and person. We have been known, as our events keep growing, to just smile at each other to communicate our joy without having to say a word.

DNation, for me, is the culmination of so much good in my life. As of this writing, I am sixty-five years old. About half the DNation members and all my staff partners have parents younger than I, including my co-chair. I am about two months older than her mother!

The final impetus for me to write this book came from crossing the finish line at the 2013 ING NYC Marathon. I was going to give up on doing that race and probably any other race due to Achilles tendonosis. But when I walked into our monthly committee meeting on October 2, 2013, I said to myself I did not belong in that room if I did not try to do the race. After that meeting, as we always do, we went out for dinner. At dinner I told everyone about my tendon issue. Wouldn't you know it? A friend told me to see a doctor who wound up creating an orthotic for me that saved my racing career.

Race day with DNation is always so rewarding. Our group runs build such a wonderful camaraderie that you relish as each member celebrates his or her personal triumph within our group triumph. So many have survived the disease themselves and are now doing the race in incredible times. Actually, any finish is an incredible time. As I love to say IF YOU FINISH IT YOU WIN IT. Many of our athletes honor loved ones either fighting and surviving the cancer, or sadly lost to the disease. As with every race, I love just stepping back often with my co-chair and looking at everyone with such pride and Gratitude for being a part of this super group of athletes and people.

Being with such a younger group has given me a different outlook on life that I am very Blessed to have. These folks are always looking to do more athletically and personally. The last thing on their minds is anything like retirement, which is normal for sixty-somethings to talk about.

When I started we were associated with the Philly Triathlon now Tri Rock Philly. There was no way I was going to be a part of an event I was not going to do. So on my sixtieth birthday, I did my first triathlon and have been doing them ever since. While I do not see myself ever doing the Iron Distance events (2.4 mile swim, 112 mile bike ride and finishing with a marathon), I have completed a Half-Iron Distance that is "only " a 1.2 mile swim followed by a fifty-six mile bike ride and concludes with a half-marathon. As a dear friend likes to say: "go big or go home." Triathlons are great events that test your endurance by having to do three events not just one. The training is hard as you have to concern yourself with three sports, but it is fun and yields a very healthy life style.

My first triathlon was one of the great days of my life. The thrill of doing something for the first time, and overcoming my fear of swimming in the Schuylkill River while loving the experience, was beyond joyous. But the real thrill for me came as I showered afterward and realized I liked the guy in the mirror.

At sixty, you have to evaluate your life. I liked the results of my evaluation, and naturally, felt very Grateful. At dinner Gail told me we were going on the March of the Living, an unbelievable two-week trip that starts with a week in Poland, seeing concentration camps followed by a week in Israel, including Israel Independence Day. It was a very special two weeks for us. While there, I decided one of my goals would be to run the Tel Aviv Full- or Half-Marathon and follow it with my favorite Israeli food: shawarma.

The triathlon community, like cycling and running, is also wonderful to be part of. In the 2013 Brigantine Triathlon, I had a bad day. Early on, I felt a myopic migraine headache coming on that I get every three months or so. As I got out of the swim (the order is always swim, bike, run) I was not happy with how I felt. On the first part of the bike I rebounded with a tail wind. Then the head wind for the second half of the bike had me struggling. As I started to run, I saw three younger guys with amazing looking physiques already finished with all three sports.

I started to meekly run by them, hoping they would not notice. They did and to my total delight not only wished me well but also made it very clear that I was one of them. A few moments later the migraine took full effect, but not before I proclaimed how I love triathlons and triathletes.

During my tenure at DNation (still ongoing), I was asked by the Golden Slipper Club and Charities to become President of the Senior Center. The Senior Center serves around 500 seniors. There are about 200 who live in a building that is full of people of very limited means and with no chance to improve their finances. Without us, many would stay in their rooms all day, watch TV, and try to scrape together something to eat. With us they get up, get dressed, come eat and have a chance to be part of a community.

Once again I was Blessed with an amazing and inspiring Executive Director, Past President and Chairperson of the Board. My initial reaction joining them was very much like when deciding to do a triathlon. It looked very daunting. With all I have been through and grown from, I took it on with the confidence I could handle it.

One of the areas I do not emphasize much is that I do not speak a lot at meetings. My feeling is if things are going well and I am a leader, then I should let others speak. I feel if you want to have power, then empower. The power I want is for success in whatever group or cause I am involved with. Somehow with the support from my Executive Director and Past President I found myself speaking up a lot more. I am now forever in their debt for the belief they have in me.

One of the activities as co-chair I often get to do, is speak to our group at our pre-race dinners and other events like the kick-offs that we hold. At ACS we naturally want to tell folks where their money goes. I have heard many wonderful people speak about the lives ACS saves and touches. I have been able to put my own spin on that and instead of citing statistics, I use the patients I see at HUP or others who come up to me to thank me for being a part of ACS. Using a story about a patient or someone else I know who was saved by a cure that was made possible in part by our money, is something I love to do. I remind everyone, after you do a race, the next day look at the people around you and remember: with the advances in cancer research that ACS has been a major part of, virtually everyone you see or one of their loved ones will owe their life to the money you raise.

Recently a motivational speaker, who happened to be sitting at my table, told me how awesome I was and gave me a big heartfelt hug. There are so many other kind words people have used to describe my speeches. It is one of the major reasons I write this book. A book can help get you speaking gigs to promote your book and ideas in it. Thank you DNation, BAT and ACS along with Golden Slipper for giving me the confidence and helping me discover me. The gift of touching people in a positive way is in every way a reason for an Attitude of Gratitude.

Chapter 22
THE GLASS IS NEITHER HALF FULL
NOR HALF EMPTY;
IT IS FULL WITH CAPACITY TO DOUBLE

As I reach the conclusion of this book, I admit to mixed emotions. I have loved every minute of writing it. It has been so much fun. My Attitude of Gratitude is off the charts for so many people I am Blessed to have in my life. While I have mentioned very few by name, to all of you in my life who are reading this book, please know you are a part of not only this book, but why I feel so happy nearly all the time.

As I hope you can see in my previous chapters, I am someone Blessed to be loving life for the most part and having An Attitude of Gratitude that lifts up people as they lift me up.

There are three things I have discovered one must have before they can truly be happy. They are life admission tickets to the party. I will label each item as they deserve to have their own separate acknowledgement:

TO TRULY LIVE
YOU MUST FORGIVE,
IF YOU CANNOT DO THAT,
AT LEAST LET GO.

First and foremost you must be able to let go of grudges and forgive. Yes, I know I have very likely not suffered how you may have suffered in cases such as child abuse, murder, physical attacks, disabilities, etc. But I can relate to you how my forgiving others has affected me and explain some of the observations I've made of people in my life for whom not forgiving has affected them.

In my late twenties, a close friend of mine announced he was finally getting married to his long-time girlfriend. He told me I would be in the wedding party and how important I was to him and his soon-to-be wife. As the date approached, I heard nothing about wedding party in spite of others telling me they were going to be part of it. Then at the wedding, Gail and I were seated at a table way in the back with people I knew he did not like, but had to invite.

I was very happy he went on a honeymoon and then got very busy with tax season (he is an accountant). One day he called me with tickets to a game. I was ready to tell him where to go with the tickets but figured why not see a game for free on his dime. I avoided dinner with him and just met him at the game. When we saw each other for the first time in months (we did speak a few times) I smiled and gave him a hug. My reason was simple: I did not want to boot him out of my life.

A couple days later, I figured out why he had treated me so badly. He was sure of my friendship, but not that of others whom he needed to advance his career. We have not seen each other much in recent years for a variety of reasons such as different life styles, but the feeling is still there. We go to at least one game per year and it is one of the most special days of the year for me. When my father passed, I called him and he told me he would be there for me. The hug he gave me helped me so much. I would not have had that had I not forgiven him.

There is also a colleague I work with, who came from a lot of money. We once discussed our backgrounds and how neither of us ever thought we would be real estate brokers considering our family's respective fortunes. He then told me he had not spoken to his parents in seventeen years due to how they "cheated him out of his inheritance." I could feel the anger and sadness in his life and now understand how unhappy he seems to be all the time.

One does not *have* to forgive someone for something that happened to them. I am not sure I could forgive someone if, G-d forbid, a loved one was killed by another. But I do know you have to

167

accept it. A friend of mine several years ago was killed by a drunk driver. The driver came from a lot of wealth and influence and somehow was on the road in spite of having other drunk-driving violations. His lawyer managed to get him out on bail. That despicable human being then left the country, leaving no doubt he would never come back or face justice for killing a wonderful person.

The mother of my friend who was killed, in honor of her son, is now very active against drunk driving. She has been an inspiration to many. She has many friends and a very loving caring family. She never forgave her son's killer, but accepted what had happened. She said of this horrible man, "I have no envy or compassion for his soul when he meets his Maker. I will not celebrate his passing, but will also not mourn in any way, shape or form." His father never overcame his justified anger and bitterness. He died less than a year after his son's premature death.

WHEN YOU LOOK FOR THE LIGHT
YOUR LIFE WILL BE BRIGHT

The second thing you need to do is to look for the positive with an ever watchful eye on evil and other problems in your life. One of the great annoyances that I feel is an impediment to Gratitude that we face every day, is the media's obsession with negativity. Do we really need to see parents' reaction on camera when their child has been brutally murdered? How many times must we see someone torn down who was once on top of the world and inspiring us all? When there is a murder trial, how many times must we hear about it in minute detail? The big question, though, is how does watching it make you feel?

For some reason, while on a ski trip with friends in Vermont a few years ago, I watched the local news. The major story was about an area couple celebrating their fiftieth wedding anniversary. They decided to eat at the same diner they had their first meal together and had ordered the same thing. The problem of the day was that the diner no longer served root-beer floats. The report went into detail about what makes up a root-beer float.

I laughed and said some words about the people watching that I am not proud of. The next day I saw every local person with a smile on his or her face. I saw the light and proudly called myself the unflattering words I had used to describe those same people the night before. The positive story spread joy. My derogatory comments did not.

With my smart phone now allowing me to hear music of my liking whenever I want, I have stopped watching news on TV unless there is something special on, like the Phillies winning a World Series or Villanova winning a national championship. I have since noticed a remarkable difference in how I feel each morning and when going to sleep. One morning, I listened to music as usual while getting ready for work, before going in to see my first appointment of the day. Meanwhile, there was some horrific murder of a child all over the news. My client described the parents' tears of grief. The look on his face told me how upset he was.

I questioned the situation. Did he have to watch it? What did he do for the victim or his/her family? What did he gain from watching it? The answers proved to me I should keep listening to music and forget about the news on TV. Do not think I am oblivious of the news. I do read online, in newspapers and watch some national news, as long as they are not doing tragedy central.

So many of my patients have shown me you can always find good in your world. Here they are with a very serious, maybe even terminal disease, with all sorts of sadness. Yet they are Grateful for doctors, nurses and their loved ones. If they can find the positives, I can find them. When I lose a deal, I look for the next one. In the case of someone difficult to deal with in any business situation, I try to think of all the great people I work with.

One can always find good or bad in any situation. About two years ago I went after some business with a very successful businessman. He had something like three major companies, all of them were making money. While I was there, his wife called about one of his kids. He became angry to the point that you could tell his day and maybe week was ruined. It seems his child only got an eighty-eight on a major test and this man was enraged. The course was honors and his kid was a sports star and otherwise a straight-A student.

I can only imagine what kind of father and husband he is. I never

169

got to find out as the deal I was hoping to work on with him never came close to fruition. About the same time, I had lunch with someone who had a child with special needs who, in all likelihood would be gone in a few years from the ailment. That man talked with such love for this child, his other kids and wife. And he did so with such joy in his voice and on his face.

One day at work, I lost two major deals. Instead of concentrating on that, I decided to think about another call I had that day. Someone who was involved with a deal I had lost earlier in the month, called to say that he had a friend looking for a real estate broker to lease some space. From the address given to me, I knew it was not something I really wanted. What made the call so special is he thanked me for being a professional and pleasure to work with during our original non-deal.

May you all be Blessed with an outlook that will always keep you focused on what you have to be Grateful for and not what you think you are lacking.

TRUST IS A MUST

As you know by now, I take my Jewish faith seriously in a spiritual sense. I believe we are created in G-d's Image and each of us is charged with the responsibility to do His Will. That is never easy to do or even understand. So many times I have prayed and while my desires were not always granted, I have always felt the Almighty heard my prayers and helped me get through whatever situation I was praying about. This book has been my personal history.

The question is, what is your faith? What do you believe your purpose in life is? What or who do you turn to in order to get through a tough time? What do you give thanks for? This does not have to be based upon a Higher Being. I have seen so-called atheists find solace in Gratitude or how expansive nature and the universe are.

Children find solace in the love of their parents. My patients find trust in doctors and nurses and their religion. Athletes, before a big game or event, will turn to their teammates, coaches and trainers. Students, the night before an exam, will often *not* cram if they have

170

followed the work all along and trust their preparation to confidently go into a big exam.

There are Jews today who are Orthodox because during the Holocaust, with so much death going on around them, they promised G-d they would become more religious if they could survive. There have been numerous other similar stories with people of other faiths as well. On a long plane ride I had a very touching discussion with a seatmate describing the loss of several teammates on a bus trip in college. At the final funeral he walked away from the crowd and went to a mountain screaming to G-d, "Why should I believe in You? You are so Powerful but could not stop this accident from killing so many so dear to me and so young?" Just then a butterfly landed on his shoulder. He cried and has kept his faith. He strives every day to do something good to honor his friends.

To be truly happy you need to believe in the power of something higher than just you. It will guide you to do deeds, which will give you positive vibes from those you meet as well as those you share your life with. When things are tough, you will have something to turn to. The more you feel Grateful for whatever you feel Grateful for, the happier you will be. You will feel Blessed and lucky.

May the Sustainer of Life always shine upon you and your loved ones so you will always feel the warm embrace of trusting in however you believe.

ACKNOWLEDGEMENTS

To those of you who do not know me, thank you so much for reading my book. It is my hope and prayer that you have found it worth your time and money. I gave you my innermost thoughts so you can be a better and happier person for all those in your life you hold dear.

I would now like to offer a first step to living with an Attitude of Gratitude. Make a list every day about what you are Grateful about. Please note, while for me that is a totally faith-based Gratitude to G-d, your gratitude is whatever works for you. I present a few examples of why I am so Grateful:

- My wife and soul mate.
- My kids, their spouse and friends, and above all my first grandchild.
- Family members who I love and like to be around and share so much history and mostly wonderful times.
- Friends who are awesome and amazing.
- Associates at work I enjoy working with.
- Brothers/sisters in the fight against cancer.
- The American Cancer Society, DNation and Bike a Thon, Golden Slipper and the Traffic Club of Philadelphia, Chamber of Commerce Southern NJ, The Society of Industrial and Office Realtors (SIOR) and all those I work with.
- My homes in Merion, PA and Ventnor City, NJ.
- Living in a climate that is 75-80% enjoyable. I admit I am not

a fan of winter but it does make warm times something to be extra Grateful for.

- Health, both physical and mental, with so many I care around and me. I pray every day for those in my life ailing in any way.
- Living in the USA and being a citizen. In so many positive ways we are the greatest nation ever. Yes, we have faults but what country does not and where would you rather live?
- The modern State of Israel.
- Adath Israel, my synagogue and my spiritual home. It is such a warm supportive place with a dynamic Rabbi, Assistant Rabbi and Canter.
- Being born in 1951. I love this era. Yes, it is the only one I know, but I am very happy in it.
- My profession as a commercial real estate broker. I do enjoy my work about 90% of the time or more.
- For my ridiculously long commute to work. If you do not have something to annoy you at the start of the day, how can you get psyched to attack the day?
- For being a member of the Pastoral Care Department at HUP.
- For being able to afford food, housing, transportation, races/rides and so much more.
- For not having food allergies.
- For all my races/rides and being able to train for them and enjoy them.
- For the Gift of public speaking.
- For the insight to know that anyone can be wonderful and to look at each person as someone who can touch my life in a positive way.
- The confidence I have that I can touch and inspire people.
- My past has had some tough times but I look upon it as a journey under the Watchful Eye of the Almighty.
- Being able to pray to G-d directly at any time and any place.
- Truly feeling that He listens.
- Not needing proof that there is a G-d. I am so Blessed to

have felt His Sheltering and Loving Presence.

- Finally, for failing to put down all that I am Blessed with. I do not believe I could ever know how many reasons I have to be Grateful for there are too many for that.

Hopefully this will help you realize all you have to be Grateful for in your life. The more you think about what you have to be Grateful for, in my humble opinion, you will be happier and more enjoyable to be around. Yes, some have more than others but we all have plenty to be Grateful for.

It is important for you to feel Grateful and happy because you matter in this world. Remember, one of my favorite Jewish sayings goes something like: *when you save a life it is as though you save the entire world and vice versa if you take a life*. The proof is simple. Think about all those in your life who you care about. How would you life feel if one of them passed away? What is it like to lose a parent, child, sibling, spouse, partner, friend, neighbor, associate, someone you do business with of any kind, someone you see every day in public, etc? Remember all the funerals you go to and how upset people are. For some, their lives will never be the same. That is proof how we all matter and are important.

Gratitude from deep personal experience will change your outlook on life and make you someone who makes worlds better. It will make your world better. Thank you for reading about my Happitude of Gratitude. May you feel it with every part of your heart, mind, body and soul.

I conclude with the daily prayer I say:

G-d thank you for all you Bless me with.
Things I acknowledge,
Things I overlook, I do not know are Blessings
And all that you Bless with I do not even know about.

Grant me Your Spirit
So I have the insight, wisdom, strength and courage
To know and perform they will,
And be with me and my loved ones and those I care about
Now and always.

May the words of my mouth
And the meditations of my heart
Be acceptable to You,
My Rock and my Redeeme

Made in the USA
Middletown, DE
04 February 2017